• Bartholomew •

WALK DORSET
AND THOMAS HARDY'S
WESSEX

Bartholomew
An Imprint of HarperCollins*Publishers*

A Bartholomew Walk Guide
Published by Bartholomew
HarperCollins*Publishers*
77-85 Fulham Palace Road
London W6 8JB

First published 1994
© Bartholomew 1994

Original research by David Perrott and Laurence Main
Design by Bob Vickers

Britain's landscape is changing all the time. While every
care has been taken in the preparation of this guide, the
Publisher accepts no responsibility whatsoever for any
loss, damage, injury or inconvenience sustained or
caused as a result of using this guide.

Printed in China

ISBN 0 7028 2562 X
94/1/15

ABOUT THIS BOOK

This is a book of walks, ranging from short, gentle strolls to more demanding hill climbs, all of which can be completed within a day. The areas covered by this guide are Dorset and the neighbouring counties of Somerset, Wiltshire and Hampshire. The countryside here inspired much of Thomas Hardy's writing and an awareness of his work will add immensely to the enjoyment of the walks.

The walks pass through every type of scenery to be found in the area – gentle, rolling hills, unspoilt heathland, sweeping chalk downs, spectacular coastal scenery, and small market towns full of historical interest. Each walk is graded according to its level of difficulty, and wherever specialist hill-walking equipment is required, this is specified.

There is a description of each walk, including information on the character and condition of the paths. In addition there is a route map to aid navigation. There is also a brief description of points of interest along the way. The location of each walk within the area is shown on the location map on page 5.

Car parks, where available, are indicated on the route maps. If it is necessary to park by the road-side, take care to avoid blocking the road, passing places or field entrances.

This guide supplies all the necessary information to complete each walk as long as the weather and visibility are good. In bad weather and low visibility, however, the use of a detailed map and compass is strongly advised on all hill routes. There is a section of advice to walkers in the introduction which you should read before setting out.

The introduction also provides a brief summary of the geography, history and wildlife of the area, plus information on rights of way, the Country Code and some useful addresses.

CONTENTS

LOCATION MAP

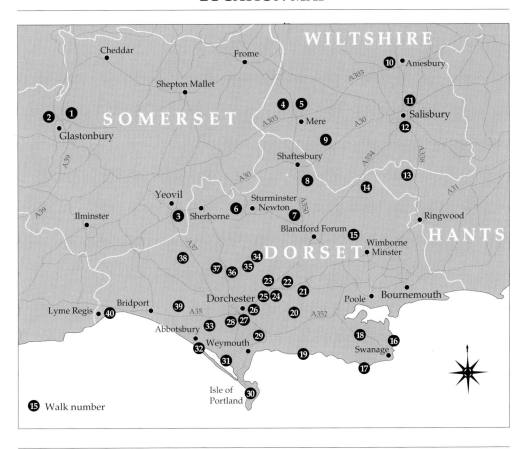

WILTSHIRE

Cheddar

Frome

Shepton Mallet

⑩ Amesbury

④ ⑤

⑪
Salisbury
⑫

SOMERSET

Mere

Glastonbury

② ①

⑨

Shaftesbury

⑧

⑬

⑭

Yeovil

Sturminster
Newton
⑥ ⑦

Ilminster

③ Sherborne

Ringwood

Blandford Forum
⑮
Wimborne
Minster

HANTS

DORSET

㊴

㊲ ㊱ ㉟ ㉞

㉓ ㉒

Dorchester
㉕ ㉔

㉑

Poole Bournemouth

Lyme Regis

Bridport

㊴

⑳

A352

㊵

A35

㉝ ㉘ ㉗

⑱

Abbotsbury

㉙

⑯

㉜ Weymouth

Swanage

㉛

⑲

⑰

Isle of
Portland

㉚

⑮ Walk number

KEY TO ROUTE MAPS

Road	❶ Route description	Viewpoint
Footpath	Ⓐ Points of interest	Woodland / forest
Route	ⓘ Information centre	Slope or crags
station Railway	Ⓟ Parking	Marsh
▲ Summit / peak	☏ Telephone	Built-up area
156 Spot height in metres	Camping / caravanning	Beach

5

INTRODUCTION

Dorset is a predominantly rural county with an amazing variety of scenery. The gentle, undulating countryside around Blackmoor Vale and the River Stour contrasts vividly with the wild heathland of mid-Dorset and the outstanding natural beauty of the rugged coastline. Rolling chalk hills with ridge-top footpaths provide splendid walking; so does the Dorset Coast Path with its huge cliffs and interesting features such as Golden Cap, Durdle Door and Chesil Beach. The county has a fascinating history too, dominated by the remains of prehistory. Hillforts, tumuli, earthworks and other ancient monuments are scattered across the countryside. There are also many delightful villages and country towns which are well worth visiting.

Thomas Hardy, the poet-novelist, was born in Higher Bockhampton in 1840. He lived most of his life in Dorset and died just outside Dorchester in 1928. He was convinced that 'it is better for a writer to know a little bit of the world remarkably well than to know a great part of the world remarkably little'. His little bit of the world was Wessex. He first adopted it in *Far from the Madding Crowd*, thus giving a territorial definition, based on the old Saxon kingdom, to unite his series of novels. Hardy's Wessex was always 'partly real, partly dream-country', but it has become a practical definition of a rare thing in England – a province. County boundaries were disregarded, while towns and villages were renamed, often transparently, giving Hardy his *own* stage, upon which his stories were set. He exploited this by demanding of his publishers that the words 'Wessex novels' head the advertising of his booklists. Hardy's Wessex became vividly detailed, making its exploration fascinating.

This book is concerned with the heart of Hardy's Wessex – Dorset and the neighbouring counties of Somerset, Wiltshire and Hampshire. Hardy's map did extend further, from the Scilly Isles to Oxford, but there is enough in this more compact area to be going on with. Lovers of Hardy's novels and poems come here from all over the world, and an awareness of his work will add immensely to the appreciation of this area, whilst enabling the walker, travelling in a way thoroughly recommended by Hardy, to really get to know 'remarkably well' this 'little bit of the world'.

1 EGDON HEATH

The landscape of Hardy's Wessex is far from uniform. Its variety is striking, from the Vale of the Little Dairies to the wilds of Egdon Heath and the inspiring Wessex Heights. Its core is Hardy's native parish of Stinsford (the 'Mellstock' of the novels). Hardy was born here in a cottage at Higher Bockhampton in 1840. This was then a wild, lonely place where 'snakes and efts swarmed in the summer days, and nightly bats would fly about our bedrooms'. The most prominent features of Hardy's boyhood environment were the Heath and the River Frome, which separates Bockhampton from the county town of Dorchester. Hardy gave the individual heaths, which extend to Poole Harbour, the collective name of Egdon Heath, where the outlook was 'lone and bare'. The wild beauty of this excited Hardy's imagination, especially in *The Return of the Native*, where Clym Yeobright 'was permeated with its scenes, with its substance, and with its odours'. In *The Mayor of Casterbridge*, Hardy described the heath as 'that ancient country whose surface never had been stirred to a finger's depth, save by the scratching of rabbits, since brushed by the feet of the earliest tribes'.

Only small pockets of this wasteland have survived the agricultural improvements and the dense conifer afforestation of the 20th century, and few seem capable of appreciating the value of such wilderness. One of the few, Christopher Booker, in a letter to *The Times* (20th February 1982) pointed out that 'this strange and unique fragment of Britain's landscape is as irreplaceable as a Gothic cathedral'. Wildlife that survives in the remaining habitats includes the lovely marsh gentian, the smooth snake and the sand lizard. The heath is a valuable habitat, with geology, climate, soil-structure and vegetation combining to form a rare character.

2 THE VALLEY OF THE GREAT DAIRIES

The River Frome flows eastwards to Poole Harbour. Its green, fertile valley was where the waters 'were as clear as the pure River of Life shown to the Evangelist, rapid as the shadow of a cloud, with pebbly shallows that prattled to the sky all day long'. Angel Clare courted Tess here, 'in the valley her spirits up wonderfully' upon first sight. This is still lush, dairy-farming landscape, although the milkmaids have been replaced by machines. Summer brings a leafy arborescence, but in the early morning, Hardy noted 'perhaps the summer fog was more general, and the meadows lay like a white sea, out of which the scattered trees rose like dangerous rocks'. Here was a rich seam from which Hardy could link the environment with human emotions, as in *Tess of the d'Urbervilles*: 'Amid the oozing fatness and warm ferments of the Froom Vale, at a season when the rush of juices could almost be heard below the hiss of fertilization, it was impossible that the most fanciful love should not grow passionate. The ready bosoms existing there were impregnated by their surroundings'. In autumn the river filled up and 'the smallest gullies were all full; there was no taking short cuts anywhere, and foot passengers were compelled to follow the permanent ways'.

3 THE VALE OF THE LITTLE DAIRIES

The Vale of Blackmore, or Blackmoor, was the home of Tess. Its gateway is Sturminster Newton, past which flows the River Stour and it is best seen from the surrounding heights. The river and its tributaries give the vale its character, enhanced by the villages which cluster on islands of higher ground above land liable to flooding. Hardy wrote in *The Woodlanders* that the Vale 'cannot be regarded as inferior to any inland scenery of the sort in the west of England, or perhaps anywhere in the Kingdom'. The heavy clay soil is the kind where Hardy felt 'superstitions linger longest'. The trees relate to humans, as in *The Woodlanders*, when Marty South remarked that the young pines she was planting seemed to 'sigh because they are very sorry to begin life in earnest – just as we be'.

4 SOMERSET

Hardy knew south Somerset well. He lived at Yeovil for a few months in 1876 and explored the surrounding countryside. The contrast between Somerset and Dorset is great, with the clay of the Somerset Levels replacing the chalk and limestone of Dorset. Here is the Vale of Avalon and Glastonbury Tor, a place of the highest significance in its own right. Perhaps this intimidated Hardy as he confined himself to poetry in this county, finding inspiration for what is said to be his most successful poem, *The Trampwoman's Tragedy*:

'Beneath us figured tor and lea,
From Mendip to the western sea –
I doubt if finer sight there be
Within this royal realm.'

5 THE CHANNEL COAST

Hardy's Wessex is not just magnificent country-side, it also has fine coastal scenery. Weymouth was only 10 miles (16 km) from Hardy's home and he was fond of 'the boats, the sands, the esplanade'. Hardy wrote *Desperate Remedies*, his first published novel, in Weymouth, but *The Trumpet Major* and *The Dynasts* are the fruits of a longer association with the coast. Hardy's grand-parents remembered when this coastline was under threat of invasion by Napoleon, and folk-memories and legends from the time enliven Hardy's works. *The Hand of Ethelberta* is the novel of Purbeck. This 'isle' is a microcosm of the Dorset landscape, with chalk, clay, limestone, sand and shale, rugged and gentle scenery. It is reached through the gap guarded by Corfe Castle which, like the cliffs and headlands of Purbeck, was visited frequently by Hardy. The newly-married Thomas and Emma Hardy walked the cliffs east of Swanage, where the detached stumps of chalk stand witness to the power of the waves. Further west, towards Weymouth, the spectacular cove at Lulworth is where Sergeant Troy was thought to have drowned in *Far from the Madding Crowd*. This military connection is reinforced by the figure of George III on horseback carved in the chalk above Osmington, as if the King were reviewing his troops (the downs were the venue of grand military reviews in Napoleonic times). Inland is the Hardy monument – to Nelson's Hardy (Sir Thomas Masterman Hardy), not the novelist. The cliffs reach their climax near the Devon border with Golden Cap, the highest cliff on the Channel coast.

6 WILTSHIRE AND HAMPSHIRE

Salisbury, the 'Melchester' of Hardy's novels, was his favourite city. It is divided from Dorset by Cranborne Chase, 'a country of ragged woodland, which, though intruded on by the plough at places, remained largely intact from prehistoric times, and still abounded with yews of gigantic growth and oaks tufted with mistletoe'. This was the symbolic background for the violent episodes in Tess's life, its 'Druidical mistletoe' heralding the concluding scene at Stonehenge. The Chase itself made Tess 'restless and uneasy' where 'she feared the unknown'. Wardour Castle, on the northern edge of the Chase, is the destination of an outing by Jude and Sue in *Jude the Obscure*. The couple were taking a trip from Salisbury, where the Training College has been attended in real life by Hardy's sister Mary and in *Jude the Obscure* by Sue Bridehead. Hardy, the trained architect, found Salisbury's Cathedral Close 'as beautiful a scene as any I know in England – or for the matter of that elsewhere'.

7 WESSEX HEIGHTS

There are no mountains in Wessex, but there are high places with magnificent views. These were Hardy's Wessex Heights, 'where men have never cared to haunt nor women have walked with me, and ghosts then keep their distance; and I know some liberty'. The north Dorset escarpment overlooking the Vale of Blackmore constantly recurs in the novels. Here is the scene of Tess's poverty-stricken winter at Flintcombe-Ash, 'a starve-acre place' where 'Tess slaved in the morning frosts and in the afternoon rains'. Not far from here is the Giant of Cerne Abbas, the 'Cernel Giant' who ate babies in ancient times, according to Mrs Cantle in *The Dynasts*. This is also sheep country and Hardy wrote of the sheep-fair at 'Greenhill' (Woodbury Hill) outside 'Kingsbere' (Bere Regis), the annual gathering on the top of a hill attended by 'multitude after multitude' of 'horned and hornless' sheep. Nearby is Tolpuddle, the home of the trade union Martyrs. Their trial was held in Dorchester, Hardy's 'Casterbridge' and the town most closely associated with the novelist. The Dorset County Museum provides a fine introduction to the area.

8 WESSEX IN HISTORY AND LEGEND

There was another Wessex which existed long before that of Thomas Hardy. It is conventionally ascribed to the West Saxons, who established themselves in the 6th century in the area south of the River Thames, including much of the modern counties of Avon, Somerset, Dorset, Wiltshire, Hampshire and Berkshire. Their leader was Cerdic of Gewissae, however, a British king regaining his patrimony.

The most famous son of the house of Wessex was Alfred the Great, who was markedly Celtic in outlook. His chosen adviser was Asser, a Welsh monk whose brother, Morgan Hen, was king of South Wales. Alfred's mentor in his youth was St Swithin, whose name is derived from Sywedydd, meaning magician, or druid.

The landscape of Wessex is littered with ancient monuments, with Stonehenge arguably the most famous in the world. Agriculture in Wessex has been dated back to 4000 BC, although there were cave dwellers here in the middle of the Ice Age, about half a million years ago. By about 500 BC, much of what was to become Wessex was the tribal territory of the Durotriges, who built impressive hillforts, such as that at Maiden Castle, just outside Dorchester. They could not stop the Romans however, who established their culture here for 400 years. The British hillfort of Old Sarum, near Salisbury, was converted into a Roman town, but Maiden Castle was abandoned in favour of a new town called Durnovaria, which became Dorchester, Hardy's 'Casterbridge'.

9 WILDLIFE

The variety in the Wessex landscape is reflected in its wildlife. The fragments of heathland left in Dorset are home to many rare plants and animals. In summer you may see an emperor dragonfly, or a silver-studded blue butterfly. The smooth snake, one of Britain's rarest reptiles, has its home on the open heathland, while a marsh gentian may be seen amidst thicker vegetation. On the limestone cliffs, in summer, look out for the adonis blue butterfly. Gulls, including kittiwakes, abound along the coast, with Portland Bill being a major bird migration point. The spring or autumn would be the best time to witness this spectacle. In summer, the swans can be seen at Abbotsbury. Poole Harbour is a feeding ground for many birds, including a large colony of black-headed gulls.

10 RIGHTS OF WAY

These walks are along rights of way. Please remember to keep to the path and always regard it as a privilege to cross someone else's land; in that way we can build an atmosphere of cooperation, rather than confrontation, in the countryside. Many of these walks cross land grazed by sheep, where dogs are not welcome. The Animals Act (1971) states that dogs endangering livestock may be shot. The Protection of Livestock Act (1953) makes it an offence to permit a dog to worry livestock, with a maximum penalty of £200. Worrying includes being at large in a field in which there are sheep. If your path is obstructed (although these routes were chosen for their lack of obstructions), contact the county council, which is the highway authority. In Dorset, you are also advised to contact the lively local Ramblers' Association, whose Area Secretary is Mr Brian Panton, 5 Nicholas Gardens, Ensbury Park, Bournemouth BH10 4BA. Tel (0202) 526954. Further information on rights of way is available from the Ramblers' Association, 1-5 Wandsworth Road, London SW8 2XX. Tel 071-582 6878.

11 THE COUNTRY CODE

Enjoy the countryside and respect its life and work.

Guard against all risk of fire.

Leave gates as you find them.

Keep your dogs under close control.

Keep to public paths across farmland.

Use gates and stiles to cross fences, hedges and walls.

Leave livestock, crops and machinery alone.

Take your litter home.

Help to keep all water clean. Protect wildlife, plants and trees.

Take special care on country roads.

Make no unnecessary noise.

12 ADVICE TO WALKERS

Always check the weather forecast before setting off on longer walks and prepare yourself accordingly. Remember that an excess of sunshine – causing sunburn or dehydration – can be just as debilitating as cold weather or rain. Carry adequate cover for your body in all conditions.

Other weather-associated danger on hills is mist or low cloud which can appear very swiftly and cut visibility to a few yards. Such conditions should be anticipated, and a map and compass carried while on higher ground.

Obviously these problems are unlikely to arise on the shorter, simpler routes, but it is always wise when out walking to anticipate the worst and to be ready for it. The extra equipment may never be needed, but it is worth taking anyway, just in case. Spare food, a first-aid kit, a whistle and a torch with a spare battery should be carried on all hill walks. In addition, details of your route and expected time of return should be left with someone, whom you should advise on your safe return.

13 USEFUL ADDRESSES

WEATHER INFORMATION

Telephone (0891) 141207 for a local weather forecast.

TRAIN AND BUS INFORMATION

British Rail's scenic line between Salisbury and Yeovil Junction is useful, while rural buses run everywhere. Services are infrequent to many places, however, so it is advisable to obtain the annual booklet *Public Transport in Rural Dorset* (published in November) from the Transportation and Engineering Department, Dorset County Council, County Hall, Dorchester, Dorset DT1 1XJ. Tel (0305) 251000. You may need to re-check these timetables locally in the summer. Frequent services on the urban fringe (particularly near Weymouth) are not included. Details of these and of bus services outside Dorset should be obtained from local tourist information centres and the bus companies:

Southern National, Edward Street, Weymouth, Dorset DT4 7BP. Tel (0305) 783645.

Wilts & Dorset: Bus Company Ltd, Bus Station, 8 Endless Street, Salisbury, Wilts SP1 1DW. Tel (0722) 336855.

Wilts & Dorset: Bus Company Ltd, Bus Station, Arndale Centre, Poole, Dorset BH15 1SN. Tel (0202) 673555.

Badgerline Ltd, Badger House, Oldmixon Crescent, Weston-Super-Mare, Avon BS24 9AX. Tel (0934) 621201.

TOURIST INFORMATION

Southern Tourist Board
40 Chamberlayne Road, Eastleigh, Hampshire SO5 5JH. Tel (0703) 620006.

West Country Tourist Board
60 St Davids Drive, Exeter, Devon EX4 4SY. Tel (0392) 76351.

Tourist information centres (Dorset):
Marsh & Ham Car Park, West Street, Blandford Forum DT11 7AW. Tel (0258) 454770.

Westover Road, Bournemouth BH1 2BU. Tel (0202) 789789.

32 South Street, Bridport DT6 3NQ. Tel (0308) 24901.

1 Acland Road, Dorchester DT1 1JW. Tel (0305) 267992.

Guildhall Cottage, Church Street, Lyme Regis DT7 3BS. Tel (0297) 442138.

The Quay, Poole BH15 1HE. Tel (0202) 673222.

8 Bell Street, Shaftesbury SP7 8AE. Tel (0747) 53514.

3 Tilton Court, Digby Road, Sherborne DT9 3LW. Tel (0935) 815341.

The White House, Shore Road, Swanage BH19 1LB. Tel (0929) 422885.

Town Hall, East Street, Wareham BH20 4NG. Tel (0929) 552740.

The King's Statue, The Esplanade, Weymouth DT4 7AN. Tel (0305) 765221.

29 High Street, Wimborne Minster BH21 1HR. Tel (0202) 886116.

Tourist information centres (Hampshire):
New Forest Museum & Visitor Centre, Lyndhurst SO43 7NY. Tel (0703) 282269.

The Furlong, Ringwood BH24 1AZ. Tel (0425) 470896.

Tourist information centres (Wiltshire):
Redworth House, Flower Lane, Amesbury SP4 7HG. Tel (0980) 623255.

Fish Row, Salisbury SP1 1EJ. Tel (0722) 334956.

Tourist information centres (Somerset):
The Tribunal, 9 High Street, Glastonbury BA6 9DP. Tel (0458) 832954.

Somerset Visitor Centre, Forte Services (A303), Podimore, Nr Yeovil BA22 8JG. Tel (0935) 841302.

Petter's House, Petter's Way, Yeovil BA20 1SH. Tel (0935) 71279.

Walk 1
GLASTONBURY TOR

2.5 miles (4 km)   Moderate

The Tor is a massive hillock which dominates the relatively flat country-side surrounding Glastonbury. The tower is all that remains of the 14th-century church of St Michael on the hilltop. The climb to its summit is relatively steep, though it is well worth it for the superb views of Glastonbury. The route also takes in Glastonbury Abbey, which is steeped in legend, and the Chalice Well, below which the Holy Grail is said to be buried and where the waters were once considered curative. Glastonbury is one of the most ancient English religious centres and is a central point for seekers of the mystical new age of Aquarius. The Glastonbury Zodiac symbolises Aquarius as a Phoenix, taking wing from Glastonbury. 'Glaston' may have been in Hardy's Outer Wessex. He visited Glastonbury on at least three occasions. In 1902 it was the destination of the cycle ride during which he composed the *Trampwoman* poem. In 1904 he cycled to Glastonbury again to spend 'a romantic day or two among the ruins'. In 1924 he witnessed the musical version of his verse-play *The Queen of Cornwall* at the Glastonbury Festival.

Route description

1 Start from the car park at the entrance to Glastonbury Abbey, next to the Town Hall in Magdalene Street. Buses (376 from Yeovil and Bristol) also stop here. Turn right past the Town Hall to Market Place, with its Cross. Turn right up High Street to the Parish Church of St John the Baptist.

2 Opposite St John the Baptist Church, turn right down a lane to Silver Street. Turn right at the end into Chilkwell Street. Turn left up Dod Lane and go straight on when the road bends left.

3 Cross a waymarked stile and walk uphill. Glastonbury Tor soon comes into view ahead above the hedge on your right. Continue through a waymarked kissing-gate and turn left along a lane to a way-marked stile in the corner ahead.

4 Cross the stile to walk with the hedge on your left to a stile ahead. Turn half-right to reach a stile giving access to a lane below the Tor. Turn left along the lane, ignoring a lane on your left, to a waymarked stile beside a gate on your right.

5 Cross the stile and follow the clear path to the summit of the Tor. Walk beside a hedge on your right to a stile, then bear right up steps. Continue along the path on the other side of the summit, down towards Glastonbury. Cross a stile in a hedge near the bottom and go ahead to a stile leading to Wellhouse Lane.

6 Turn left to Chilkwell Street, where you turn right. After 30 yards (27 m), you will see the Chalice Well on your right. Continue along Chilk-well Street to a fork, before continuing up Bere Lane and turning right along Fishers Hill back to the start.

Points of interest

A Visit the Glastonbury Tribunal to see the find from the prehistoric Glastonbury Lake Village.

B St John's Church has the Holy Thorn tree in its churchyard from which sprigs are sent each Christmas to the Queen and Queen Mother.

C Glastonbury Tor was thought to be in William Blake's mind when he wrote: 'And did those feet in ancient time walk upon England's mountains green?'

D The Chalice Well is held in the beak of the phoenix – the Aquarian Water-Carrier. Joseph of Arimathea is said to have hidden the chalice containing Christ's blood here. The water is stained crimson by algae.

E The Somerset Rural Life Museum is housed in the old abbey barn.

F Glastonbury Abbey is believed to have been built on the site of the wattle church built by Jesus Himself.

11

Walk 2
WEARYALL HILL

4 miles (6.4 km) Moderate

This is a pleasant walk over Wearyall Hill with views stretching over Exmoor, the Quantocks and the Mendips. The hill is surrounded by history, myth and legend, and the route takes you across holy ground as the hill is thought by many to be the home of the Holy Thorn. The sanctity of the Holy Thorn was said to be recognised even by the animal kingdom. One old Somerset legend tells of a man making a pilgrimage to it and returning with a single thorn which he planted near his home. It soon grew and the villagers were amazed to witness all the farm animals gathering around it just before midnight on Christmas Eve, accompanied by the pilgrim. At the stroke of midnight, under the light of a full moon, the beasts knelt to the Holy Thorn, now in blossom. Hardy based a poem on this tale.

"If someone said on Christmas Eve, 'Come, see the oxen kneel, In the lonely barton by yonder combe Our childhood used to know,' I should go with him in the gloom, Hoping it might be so."

Walk 2   WEARYALL HILL

Route description

1 Start from the car park at the entrance to Glastonbury Abbey, which is next to the Town Hall in Magdalene Street. Buses (376 from Yeovil and Bristol) also stop here. Turn left, then right at the A39 to Street.

2 Turn left through the swing gate waymarked 'Wearyall Hill'. Veer right uphill to a stile in the hedge at the top. **Don't cross it!** Turn right along the ridge path ignoring the track going off to the left. Carry on up the hill passing the Holy Thorn on your left. Go ahead to a stile and continue past houses on your left. Look for a stile on your left.

3 Cross on to the road and turn right. At the end of Roman Way cross the A39, just before Pons Perilis (Pomparles Bridge).

4 Go over a waymarked stile to walk with the River Brue on your left. Look for the stone marking the site of St Bride's well.

5 Turn left over a bridge and walk with the river now on your right.

6 When you reach an old bridge that used to carry the now dismantled Somerset and Dorset Railway ('the dear old S&D – Slow & Dirty') across the River Brue, look first for stone walls in the bank downstream. These show where an aqueduct used to take canal barges over the river by means of locks. Cross over the old railway bridge. Turn left immediately to a gate, then right to follow the course of the old canal.

7 Go ahead over a gate to a lane and continue through the gate opposite. Walk with the course of the old canal still on your right. Cross a footbridge ahead and continue to cross a stile beside a gate. Turn right along a lane, bear left over a bridge and pass a factory on your left.

Points of interest

A The thorn tree here is believed to be one of several descendants of the original Holy Thorn which survive in Glastonbury, said to mark the spot where Joseph of Arimathea planted his staff. It took root and burst into flower, thus signalling the end of the saint's long journey. A puritan fanatic cut the original tree down, but not before it had provided cuttings. It is considered significant that Joseph's weary band halted on Wearyall Hill, which represents a 'fish', the symbol for Pisces, in the Glastonbury Zodiac (field patterns which outline the signs of the Zodiac, when seen from high above).

Wearyall Hill also symbolises the Celtic Salmon of Wisdom and is the King Fisherman's Castle of Arthurian legend. Joseph was the old Fisher-King, arriving as a key-witness to the Resurrection at a time when the local Silures king, Arviragus, was under pressure from the Romans, who had just massacred the druids in Anglesey. Arviragus recognised the resurrected 'Salmon of Knowledge' by granting Joseph the 12 hides (or 12 Hidden Figures of the Zodiac) at Glastonbury.

Joseph was also a tin-trader. Tin is the metal of Jupiter, which is the ruling planet of Pisces. Joseph's association with this area was a long one. Many believe he sailed with Anne, the British princess, to Palestine, where she gave birth to the Virgin Mary. Jesus is thought by many to have come here with his uncle to visit his relations. He was also recognised by the druids as the promised and expected god Esse.

B Pons Perilis, or Pomparles Bridge, is the Perilous Bridge of Arthurian legend. Here the initiate passed from life to death to rebirth, in a supreme test of courage.

C Notice the stone marking the site of St Bride's well. This Celtic saint lived nearby at Old Beckery.

D In one old Somerset legend, King Arthur was commanded by an angel to go to the hermitage on Beckery Knoll. This was a place of pilgrimage because St Bride had lived there. He was offered the body of the Christ-child by Mary herself. He consumed the Holy Child, who reappeared whole on the altar.

E The canal that crossed the river here was opened in 1833, but closed in 1854.

F The soil in these disused allotments should be fertile. This was the town's septic pond in the Middle Ages.

G Glastonbury Abbey lies between the Zodiac signs for Pisces and Aquarius. The abbey was built over the original wattle church, said to have been built by Jesus and restored by Joseph of Arimathea. Encased in lead, for protection, by St David in 546, it was destroyed by a fire in 1184. The Tomb of 'Arthur' dug up by the monks in 1191 (at Henry II's behest) was actually that of Prince Iestyn, the 11th-century traitor prince of South Wales.

Walk 3
JACK THE TREACLE EATER

3.5 miles (5.6 km)   Moderate

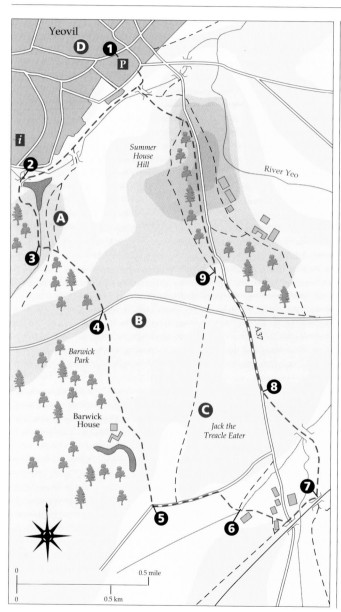

This is a varied, interesting walk on the edge of Yeovil. It passes through parkland laid out in an informal style and includes a woodland walk. Yeovil Junction Station is about half way round the walk, so British Rail travellers should join the circle at point 7. The route is clear and way-marked with yellow arrows on wooden posts. This was an initiative of the South Somerset District Council. Yeovil itself is worth visiting on completion of the walk.

Route description

1 Park your car at the Old Station car park at the south of Yeovil town centre. Start walking along the gravel path at the rear right-hand corner of the car park. Join a tarmac lane, then fork right to pass a play area on your left.

2 Cross a bridge, turn left and cross a second bridge to follow the path uphill, bearing left below a low wall to follow a level path (ignoring turnings downhill and uphill) until you reach a little waterfall.

3 Ford the stream above the waterfall on your left and when you reach railings bear left to go through a kissing-gate. Follow the broad track uphill to a kissing-gate at the top. Go ahead with the hedge on your left.

4 Go through a kissing-gate, cross a road and continue over a stile signposted 'Barwick'. Pause to see the Fish Tower on your left. Go ahead across this field to a way-marked stile. Bear left to reach a stile giving access to the drive of Barwick House. Turn left, passing a lake on your right.

5 Turn left when you reach a road, pausing to notice Jack the Treacle Eater's arch in the parkland on your left. After 300 yards (270 m), turn right through a metal gate waymarked 'Yeovil Junction' and continue straight ahead. Cross a low fence and follow the way-marked track down between hedges. Pass a bungalow on your left and look for a wooden foot-bridge to cross the stream ahead on your right.

6 Go over the stile above the footbridge and cross a field to another stile. Turn left to follow the path past the backs of houses to a road. Cross over and follow the lane towards Yeovil Junction Station.

7 Turn left through a gate before the station to follow a track above a river on your left. Look for a concrete bridge on your left. Cross the river and go straight ahead across a field to rails in a gap in the hedge ahead of you to your right.

8 Turn right along the road. Pass a road turning on your left, then 300 yards (270 m) later, bear left up a track signposted 'Round House'. Look carefully for a path through

the trees on your right after about 60 yards (55 m), waymarked 'Yeovil Old Station'.

9 Follow the path through the woods. When you reach a stile walk down an open field, bearing left to a stile and bridge to the car park.

Points of interest

A   Nine Springs, at the bottom of Hendford Hill, were landscaped in the 18th century by the owners of Aldon House. Nine springs flow into an enchanting lake and little waterfalls drop down a tiny valley.

B   The Fish Tower is one of the 18th-century follies of Barwick Park. George Messiter supposedly built them to provide work for unemployed glove-makers.

C   This folly, an archway, is named after one of Messiter's young workmen who ate treacle to sustain him on several trips to London.

D   Yeovil is a relatively busy industrial centre nowadays, although until the 18th century it was a small market town. It is famous for its glove-making indus-try which goes back over 300 years. It was in fact glove-making which

brought prosperity to Yeovil. Sheep grazing on the Dorset downland provided high-quality sheepskins for gloves. The trade still survives today and Yeovil produces gloves for shops all over the world. The town centre is worth visiting, main-ly for its impressive Ham-stone church which contains a 15th-century brass lectern and an interesting War Memorial window. Hendford Manor House nearby houses Yeovil Museum and has a noted collection of firearms and local Roman finds. On the western side of the town is Abbey Farm with its medieval Ham-stone tithe barn. Also to the west is Montacute House, a fine 16th-century mansion built of Ham stone. South-east of the main railway station is Newton Surmaville, a 17th-century manor house. The quarry of Hamdon Hill, to the west of Yeovil, provides the golden Ham Hill limestone which is used in many of the town's build-ings. An Iron Age fort stands on the hill, from where there are extensive views across the River Yeo valley. Babylon Hill, east of the town centre, also offers a good viewpoint of the surrounding countryside and of Yeovil itself.

Walk 4
ALFRED'S TOWER

5.5 miles (9 km)   Easy

The walk to Alfred's Tower affords fine views over the counties of Somerset, Dorset and Wiltshire. Built in 1772, this magnificent landmark stands at 160 feet (48 m) and is said to mark the spot where Alfred the Great raised the standard in 878 to repel the invading Danes.

Route description

1 Park opposite the entrance to Stourhead House and Gardens in the village of Stourton, just off the B3092, 3 miles (4.8 km) north-west of Mere (on the A303). An infrequent bus service (no. 20) operates from Gillingham, which is the nearest station (Tel Maiden Bradley 339 for times). Follow the path downhill from the reception building to the Spread Eagle Inn.

2 Continue along the road, passing Garden Lake on your right. Go under the rock arch and turn right to follow the public footpath to Alfred's Tower.

3 Pass a cottage on your right, followed by a fenced wood on your right as you go ahead along the clear track. Cross a stile beside a gate ahead.

4 Continue through the upper, waymarked gate. Ignore a track on your left and go ahead across a stile beside a gate to walk with conifers on both sides. Ignore side paths and ascend towards a road.

5 Turn left along a path parallel to the road to reach Alfred's Tower.

6 Follow the blue waymarker to walk parallel with the road. Turn right along the forest track to descend into Six Wells Bottom at St Peter's Pump. Walk down towards Stourhead Gardens.

7 Follow the waymarks to climb out of the valley. Pass the obelisk and follow the track back to Stourhead House and the car park.

Points of interest

A St Peter's Church, Stourton, dates from at least the 13th century.
B This rock arch carries visitors to Stourhead Gardens over the public road.

C Notice the Cascade, which was engineered in 1766.
D Henry Hoare, the enthusiast antiquarian responsible for what we now see at Stourhead, was reading about Alfred the Great in Voltaire's L'Histoire Générale when he decided to crown his scheme with a tower on Kingsettle Hill. The tower was designed by Henry Flitcroft and was completed in 1772. For opening times, check at the reception building or telephone (0747) 840348.
E St Peter's Pump was erected in 1768 and marks the spot of the first springs of the River Stour.
F The obelisk was erected originally in 1746.
G Stourhead House is open to the public from 12.00 to 17.30 daily (except Thursday and Friday) from April to October.

16

Walk 5
WHITE SHEET HILL

7.5 miles (12 km)   Easy

This is a straightforward route to a fine viewpoint at a height of 810 feet (246 m). It links with Walk 4 (Alfred's Tower) and with a visit to Stourhead. A wide, clear track leads over the chalk downland to an ancient hillfort.

Route description
1 Park in the National Trust car park opposite the entrance to Stourhead House and Gardens in the village of Stourton, just off the B3092, 3 miles (4.8 km) north-west of Mere (on the A303). There is an infrequent bus service (no. 20) from Gillingham, which is the nearest station (Tel Maiden Bradley 339 for bus times). Starting from the reception building, walk up the main drive towards Stourhead House. Look out for orange waymarkers and follow them towards Drove Lodge. Turn left along the B3092.
2 When you reach a house on your left, turn right through a gate up a hedged track. Ignore side tracks and walk uphill towards trees. Go ahead through a gate to walk with the hedge on your left to another gate. Continue uphill with a fence on your right. Ignore a stile on your right and a lane on your left, but cross a stile ahead into the nature reserve.

3 Follow a fence on your right uphill to a stile ahead. Cross this and bear right, passing two disc barrows on your right. Go ahead to the triangulation point (Ordnance Survey pillar) opposite the TV mast on the Iron Age earthwork of White Sheet Castle.
4 Follow the orange waymarks past the circular earthwork and the Neolithic Enclosure. Follow the orange arrows past an 18th-century milestone to join a lane. Follow this to the Red Lion Inn.
5 Cross over the road and continue along the lane. Look out for the orange markers and follow them across National Trust farmland. Cross a lane.
6 Go up the driveway to Home Farm. Follow the track around the side of the farm. The path leads towards Terrace Lodge where you will meet with the Lodge Driveway leading back to Stourhead House and the car park. Stourhead House definitely deserves a visit.

Points of interest
A Stourhead House is in the care of the National Trust. It was built in the 1720s by Henry Hoare I, the banker son of a Lord Mayor of London, and contains some fine Chippendale furniture. The glorious gardens were created by Henry Hoare II.
B The small, oval earthwork on your left as you cross the final stile is of Neolithic (New Stone Age) date, being constructed in about 2500 BC. It may have been a gathering place and a religious site.
C White Sheet Castle is an Iron Age hillfort. A single rampart and ditch sufficed on its south and west sides, where there are steep slopes giving natural protection, but three banks and ditches are present on the north and east sides, facing the level plateau. There is also a cross-dyke 440 yards (400 m) to the north. White Sheet refers to the steep, chalky slope of this hillside.
D Long Lane was an ancient trade route from Cornwall.

Walk 6
STURMINSTER NEWTON

4.5 miles (7 km) **Easy**

This is an easy walk across gentle countryside with pleasant views over Blackmoor Vale. The route passes along riverside meadows and through delightful wooded areas full of flora and fauna. Sturminster Newton itself is a small market town tucked into a bend of the River Stour. It takes its name from its church (minster) on this river. The locals know it as Stur and it is the gateway to the Vale of Blackmoor, a wide clay vale watered by deep springs in a narrow band of green-sand soil at the foot of the steep chalk. Sturminster Newton was Hardy's 'Stourcastle' and the place has retained the atmosphere of a small market town of Hardy's Wessex. The novelist lived here from July 1876 to March 1878, describing them as the happiest two years of his married life with Emma. Hardy wrote *The Return of the Native* here, plus several poems.

Route description
1 Park in the free Station Road car park off the B3091. Follow the main road through the town centre. Just beyond the market cross, turn left at a 'To the Church' notice. After a few yards, turn right along a lane to the church. Bear left of the church and at a T-junction beyond it, turn left between houses to a lane. Turn right then left along the track signposted Fiddleford Mill and Fiddleford Manor.

18

2 Climb a waymarked stile and bear right to follow a path across the fields. Cross a stile and continue. Turn left over a footbridge and bear right to go through a kissing-gate. Cross two more footbridges over the river and continue to a mill. Turn right by the mill to continue along a tarmac lane to a road.

3 Turn right and just after crossing a bridge over the stream, turn left at a footpath sign to climb a stile beside a metal gate. Walk uphill, keeping the fence and hedge on your right. Climb two stiles and continue along the right-hand edge of the next field with woodland on your right. Before reaching the corner of the field, turn right over a stile signposted Broad Oak to enter Piddles Wood. Some of this woodland is leased as a nature reserve to the Dorset Trust for Nature Conservation. Look out for newly planted areas of oak and wild cherry. Follow a track through the wood, and at a fork take the left-hand track. Follow signs to Broad Oak until you reach a lane.

4 Turn right along the lane and at a T-junction cross the road and turn left along a track that leads to a waymarked kissing-gate. Go through and turn half-right to follow a path across a field, soon joining and keeping by a hedge on the right. Go through a kissing-gate and continue between trees down to cross a footbridge. Head uphill to a lane and immediately turn sharp right onto a narrow, hedge-lined path. Cross a stile, bear right and, walking with the fence on your right, make for a metal gate in front of you.

5 Go through the gate; keep ahead across rough pasture. Cross a stile and continue along the right-hand edge of the pasture. Climb a stile and head down steps, turning sharp right down to the road opposite Town Bridge.

6 Turn left and then turn right down to the mill. Go round the side of the mill, cross two footbridges and turn left to go through a kissing-gate. Follow a path across more riverside meadows, go through a kissing-gate and continue along the left-hand edge of a recreation ground. Go through another kissing-gate to the left of a large house.

7 Continue past the house and descend, bearing slightly right to climb a stile. Turn right and head uphill by a hedge and fence on your right. Bear right to a kissing-gate. Go through it onto a tarmac drive and follow this back to the centre of Sturminster Newton.

Points of interest

A Fiddleford Mill is a former corn mill. It is no longer working, but it still contains some of its machinery.

B Fiddleford Manor dates back to the 14th century. It is administered by English Heritage and is open to the public during the summer months.

C Town Bridge was built in the late 15th century and was widened in the 17th century. The arched causeway approach was added in the 18th century. It bears a metal plaque threatening deportation to anyone damaging the bridge.

D The existence of watermills at Sturminster is recorded in the Domesday Survey of 1086. It is likely that one of these was the predecessor of the present mill. Sturminster Newton Mill is one of the few remaining watermills in Dorset. The majority of the mill building is late 17th century and was restored to full working order in 1981 by the Mill Trust. It is open to the public during the summer months. Notice the flood level markings on the main door from 1756 and 1979.

E Hardy brought his wife, Emma, to Riverside Villa in July 1876. This was one of a semi-detached pair of houses overlooking the River Stour. One of these houses now bears an engraved slate plaque to commemorate their two-year tenancy, but it is probably attached to the wrong one. Hardy often walked across Colber Bridge, which was erected in 1841. One of his poems was entitled *On Sturminster Footbridge*. Hardy remarked on the river's 'fishy smell from the numerous eels and other fish beneath'. Hardy indulged his love of rowing on the Stour, while his house enjoyed famous sunsets. When he returned here in 1916, after Emma's death, Hardy described Riverside Villa as her 'musical box'.

F Sturminster Newton Museum is in the old Union Work House Chapel on Bath Road. It houses exhibits on local history from pre-Roman times. Open Easter to September; 14.00-16.30 Mon & Thur, 11.00-13.00 Sat, 15.00-17.00 Sun.

Walk 7
HOD HILL

3 miles (4.8 km)   Moderate

This is a very attractive walk leading to one of several hillforts guarding the valley of the River Stour. The footpath round the base of Hod Hill is considered to be one of the prettiest paths in Dorset and the views throughout the walk are wonderful. Its name is of some significance to ley-hunters and followers of Alfred Watkins' old straight tracks. Hod recalls the box carried on the shoulder with the aid of a rod – the staff of the original surveyors of these ancient earthworks. These unploughed slopes are rich in flora and fauna; the riverside walk is a special treat.

Route description

1 Start from the White Horse pub on the A350 in Stourpaine, 2 miles (3.2 km) north-west of Blandford Forum. Park beside the White Horse or in the village. The X13 and 139 buses stop here. Turn left from the White Horse and left again down South Holme. Go ahead across Manor Road to Havelins, the road opposite, which crosses the River Iwerne.

2 Turn right up Hod Drive, the track signposted 'Bridleway to Hanford'. Pass beneath Hod Hill on your right and beside the River Stour on your left. The path can be very muddy in places.
3 Bear right with the track through trees to a road. Turn right just before the road to climb up to a gate signposted 'Hod Hill'. Walk uphill with the trees on your right.
4 Cross the stile beside a gate ahead to enter the hillfort at the corner used by the Romans. Explore all of the fort as you make for the bottom left-hand corner.
5 Cross a stile by a gate and descend along the hedged track back to Stourpaine, walking beside the River Iwerne at the foot of the hill. Turn right along Manor Road and retrace your steps to your car, or the bus stop, from the crossroads.

Points of interest
A The western side of Hod Hill, overlooking the Stour valley, is the steepest side, requiring only a low bank to defend its summit.
B When the Romans captured the Iron Age hillfort of Hod Hill in either AD 43 or 44, Vespasian's Second Legion Augusta built its own fort in the north-western corner and highest part of the British camp. It was garrisoned by 600 legionary infantry and an auxiliary cavalry unit of 250 men and their horses.
C Hod Hill is one of the largest of the Dorset hillforts, with an internal area of 54 acres (21.9 ha). It was developed over the whole of the Iron Age, with ditches and ramparts being added to make it impregnable until the Romans brought their lethal ballista machine to it on a movable siege-tower and rained ballista bolts on the Durotrigic chieftain's hut. Slight depressions in the ground indicate other British huts set alight by Roman fire arrows.

Walk 8
MELBURY BEACON

5 miles (8 km)   Moderate

Melbury Beacon, which has an old Iron Age earthwork around its summit, provides some of the finest views in Dorset. Passengers from the X13 (Shaftesbury-Bournemouth) bus can start this walk at Compton Abbas.

Route description

1 Start from the car park near the summit of Spread Eagle Hill on a minor road 2 miles (3.2 km) south of Shaftesbury, past the village of Melbury Abbas. The car park is on your right as you go south, and a stile from it invites you onto National Trust land at Fontmell Down. Go ahead, with a fence on your left.

2 Cross an old dyke and continue past a stile in the fence on your left. When you reach the end of the trees on your left, veer right downhill, passing an old parish boundary stone.

3 Go through a gate near the foot of the hill and walk along the left-hand edge of the field to the fence ahead. Turn right to walk with the fence on your left. Cross a stile and continue.

4 Go through a small gate at the end of the field to follow an enclosed path which bears left to a lane in the village of Compton Abbas. Turn right along this lane.

5 Fork right and then follow the lane around a sharp left bend to turn right at a T-junction towards East Compton. Visit the remains of

St Mary's Church, with its old cross, on your left.

6 Continue along the lane, which bends to the left and reaches the A350 after 600 yards (549 m). **Take great care** as you turn right along this main road for 250 yards (229 m) past Apple Lynchet and Whitehall Cottage.

7 Turn right along a track, then pass through a gate to follow a track which gradually climbs beside a hedge and fence on your right to a gate. The track soon bends left uphill. Go straight up, through a second gate, to the Ordnance Survey trig point at the summit of Melbury Hill. This is the site of the old beacon.

8 Continue across a stile and turn right, with Shaftesbury away on your left. Follow the fence on your right and walk down to a stile beside a gate ahead. Continue with the fence on your right. Go through a gate in the fence and walk ahead to join a track. Continue downhill passing through three gates until you reach a lane. Turn left.

9 As the lane bends sharp right, go ahead to walk up a lane marked 'unsuitable for motors'. This lane leads back to the car park.

Points of interest

A Fontmell Down is rich in butterflies and chalkland flora. This part is owned by the National Trust.

B The 15th-century church of St Mary's in East Compton was demolished in 1867. Notice the gargoyles, and the steps of the old cross in the churchyard.

C Melbury Beacon is 862 feet (263 m) high and affords magnificent views north to Shaftesbury and east over Cranborne Chase.

Walk 9
OLD WARDOUR CASTLE

4 miles (6.4 km) Easy

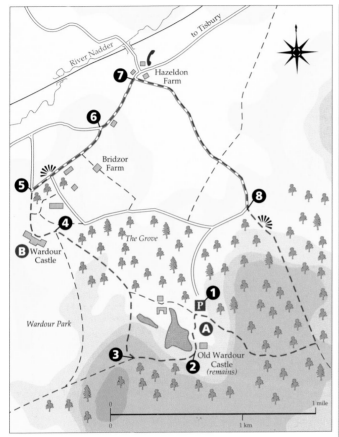

Route description

1 Start from the car park at Old Wardour Castle. This is signposted 2 miles (3.2 km) south-west of Tisbury and 1.5 miles (2.4 km) north of the A30 road between Wilton and Shaftesbury. Walk along the track with the castle on your left and the lake on your right.

2 This track soon bends right, with trees across the field on your left.

3 Fork right along the fenced track. When this track bends right to farm buildings, keep straight on over a stile with the fence on your right.

4 Go through a gate ahead to follow the crescent driveway past Cranborne Chase school on your left. Follow the driveway to the road.

5 Turn right along this road. When the road turns right, keep straight on along the private road, which is a public footpath.

6 Go ahead along the minor road, which joins your path from the left.

7 Turn right along the lane and continue along it for half a mile (0.8 km).

8 Bear left up a track to 'Fox Farm'. The forest is on your right, while there are extensive views across Nadder Valley on your left. When the track bends right to a house, continue straight ahead through conifer plantations.

9 Immediately after a track joins yours from the left, turn right. Go straight across a track to follow a fenced path between two fields. Bear right with this path through woodland (ignore a path coming from your right). Continue under an arch to walk with a fence on your left. Emerge from the wood back at the car park, with the castle on your left.

This is a walk with extensive views in one of the least spoilt parts of Wiltshire, close to the northern limit of Cranborne Chase. You can start from the car park at Old Wardour Castle. Alternatively, an excellent way to reach here is by train, on the scenic route between Salisbury and Yeovil. Alight at Tisbury and walk along the minor road south-west of the town, going under the railway bridge and bearing right. This brings you to point **7** on our walk. This is also the place to start if you come by bus (no. 26 Salisbury-Shaftesbury service). As you enjoy the view to the north, towards Fonthill, think of Sue and Jude in Hardy's *Jude the Obscure*, walking across the 'open country, wide and high' to a station on another line, 'about seven miles off to the north'. This was most probably Boyton (now closed) on the Salisbury-Westbury line. A pleasant woodland path completes the circle back to Old Wardour Castle.

Points of interest

A Old Wardour Castle is French in style, and was built in 1393 on the model of the Château de Concressault by John, 5th Lord Lovel, a veteran of the Hundred Years War. His family only lived in the castle for about 60 years. As Lancastrians they forfeited their property on the accession of Edward IV.

The site is indeed old, with King Alfred the Great probably having a royal manor here. He may have granted it to Wilton Abbey, as its nuns were the overlords of Wardour from at least Domesday Book to the 16th century. Sir Matthew Arundell purchased the property in 1570 and began to rebuild the castle in 1578. His son, Thomas Arundell, was raised to the peerage as Baron Arundell of Wardour by James I in 1605.

The Arundells were renowned for their Roman Catholicism, so it comes as no surprise to find Wardour the scene of bitter fighting in the Civil War. Sir Edward Hungerford led 1300 Parliamentarian troops against the castle's garrison of 25 men, aided by a number of female servants, in April 1643. In the absence of her husband (in Oxford with the King), Lady Blanche Arundell led the castle's resistance until 8th May. Lord Arundell's grandchildren were captured and forced to receive a Puritan education in Essex. Having spitefully destroyed the orchards and fish-ponds, the Parliamentarians then held the castle with a garrison of cavalry and infantry under Edmund Ludlow. The Royalists were strong in Wiltshire, however, while Lord Arundell sought the return of his property. The situation dragged on until 18th March 1644, when lack of food forced Ludlow to surrender.

The castle was never repaired. After the Restoration, the Arundells built a small house on the south side of the curtain wall and the castle was left as a ruin, to be surrounded by formal gardens in the 18th century. The then Lord Arundell built a totally new house a mile to the north-west, to be known as Wardour Castle.

The castle has a superb lakeside setting. Its romantic ruins and surrounding parkland were land-scaped in the late 18th century. The castle's tall, hexagonal shape now stands in harmony with tall trees, while the Gothic-style banqueting house built beside the curtain wall has been restored. The castle is in the care of English Heritage and is open daily from April to September and on winter weekends.

B A new Wardour Castle was built to the Palladian design of James Paine between 1768 and 1776. At this time Paine was a leading architect in England.

The new Wardour Castle consists of a three-storey central block with a two-storey wing on either side. In the west wing is the Church of All Saints.

The fine art collection was dispersed after the death of the last Earl of Arundell in 1944. The family then sold the (new) castle to a religious order for conversion into a seminary. This caused the stripping out of the decorated ceilings and wall-panelling. Since 1960, the castle has housed a girl's school, but it is open on Mondays, Wednesdays, Fridays and Saturdays in the summer holidays.

This is the place visited by Sue and Jude, as Hardy recorded; 'Tomorrow is our grand day, you know. Where shall we go?' 'I have leave from three till nine. Wherever we can get to and come back from in that time. Not ruins, Jude – I don't care for them'. 'Well Wardour Castle. And then we can do Fonthill if we like – all in the same afternoon.'

Walk 10
STONEHENGE

7 miles (11.2 km)   Easy

Set in the middle of Salisbury Plain, Stonehenge is the finest Bronze Age sanctuary in Europe. This is a walk along a ley line past one of the most famous of Bronze Age cemeteries.

If you rely on public transport you may prefer to take a bus to Amesbury and start on Stonehenge Road (see direction **6**) as there is only an infrequent bus service to Stonehenge (no. 3 from Salisbury). The path through the wood near direction **4** may be muddy in wet weather, but the wood itself is a haven for wildlife.

Hardy realised the drama of the scenery and made Stonehenge the conclusion of Tess's flight with Angel after the killing of Alec d'Urberville. Here, Tess appeared as the ritual sacrifice, fulfilling her own prophecy: 'Once victim, always victim – that's the law!' As Tess slept, Angel watched the black cloud of night lift 'like the lid of a pot, letting in at the earth's edge the coming day. . . . The band of silver paleness along the east horizon made even the distant parts of the Great Plain appear dark and near; and the whole enormous landscape bore that impress of reserve, taciturnity, and hesitation which is usual just before day'.

Route description

1 Start from the car park at Stonehenge, on the A344, 2 miles (3.2 km) west of Amesbury. Turn right along the A344, then turn left up a fenced track to the A303. Turn left to reach a waymarked gate on your right. Walk from Stonehenge down a fenced track.

2 Bear left with the wide track to walk with trees across the field on your right. Ignore a track from the right, but keep left to a farm. Bear left along the farm track before bending right with it.

3 Turn left at a road (in Wilsford). When you see a post box in a wall on your left, turn right to walk down a gated and fenced lane. Just before the end of this lane, turn left over a stile beside a gate and bear right, ignoring stiles on your right, to reach a footbridge over the Avon.

4 Go through a gate to cross a second footbridge over the Avon and bear right into a wood. The path goes beside a stream on your left to a footbridge. Cross this and turn left. Follow a track to a gate ahead, but **don't go through it**.

5 Turn right to walk with the fence on your left. Pass a chalk pit crowned by a disc barrow on your right. Turn left at the end of this field and go through a kissing-gate beside a gate to walk along a fenced track which bends left as it climbs. Cross a track to go through a gate ahead signposted 'Amesbury 1'. Walk down to a signposted gate and a footbridge over the Avon.

6 Cross a second and a third footbridge to go ahead past houses on your left and a cemetery on your right, to emerge at Stonehenge Road. Turn left to reach the A303. Fork right along the A344 back to Stonehenge and the car park.

Points of interest

A This old straight track is one of the leys or earth-energy lines that converge at Stonehenge. It continues straight ahead from Stonehenge when our path bends left after 1 mile (1.6 km).

B The round barrows on both sides of the track are the Bronze Age burial mounds of Normanton Down. One barrow (at the western end of the line) was excavated in 1808 and found to contain a skeleton of a 'tall and stout man', a bronze axe, a spearhead, a dagger (the wooden dagger handle was decorated with tiny gold pins), a gold breastplate, a belt hook and a polished stone macehead with an elaborately decorated handle.

C Three ley lines cross at this disc barrow.

D Stonehenge is the most famous prehistoric monument in Britain, if not in the world. It was started 5000 years ago and the reason for its construction has been lost in the mists of time. There have been countless explanations proffered, however, while the site has been the object of all kinds of research. The major axis of Stonehenge was definitely aligned with the sun at the summer and winter solstices.

The name is of Saxon origin, meaning 'hanging stones', referring to the stone lintels, which make this unique among the stone circles of Albion. Although about half of the original stones are missing, the plan is clear. An outer circle of 30 sarsens (supporting lintels) encloses a circle of bluestones (about 60 originally). Inside this are five sarsen 'trilithons' (two uprights supporting a horizontal lintel) arranged in a horseshoe shape, with its open end towards the north-east, where the midsummer sun rises. Then there is an inner horseshoe of bluestones (19 originally). The 'Altar Stone' lies at the apex of the horseshoe. The 'Slaughter Stone' lies on the midsummer sun axis on the causeway which breaks the bank and ditch encircling the monument at this crucial point. Also near this axis but further out, almost on the modern perimeter fence and the A344, stands the 'Heel Stone'.

The erection of the stones was a major operation:

Phase I, circa 2500 BC: the ditch and bank were constructed, with a ring of small pits inside containing cremation burials. Upright stones formed the entrance.

Phase II, circa 2100 BC: a double circle of bluestones were brought from the Preseli Hills in Dyfed. The entrance was modified and the avenue leading up from the banks of the River Avon was built.

Phase IIIa, circa 2075 BC: the bluestones were removed, the site was levelled and the sarsen stones were brought from Fyfield Down, near Marlborough. They were erected in an outer ring with lintels and an inner horseshoe.

Phase IIIb, circa 1700 BC: some of the bluestones were set along the line of the present inner bluestone horseshoe.

Phase IIIc, circa 1500 BC: the bluestones were reset in a ring between the two lines of sarsens and in an inner horseshoe, with the largest bluestone set upright in the centre. This is the stone that is now known as the 'Altar Stone'.

The task of erecting them must have been a huge one – the larger stones weigh over 50 tons each. Massive stone lintels were mortice-and-tenoned to these uprights and are curved to follow the circumference of a circle.

Most of the missing stones disappeared from the Middle Ages onwards when the monument was used as a quarry.

Stonehenge is open daily (admission charge).

Walk 11
OLD SARUM

4.5 miles (7.2 km)   Easy

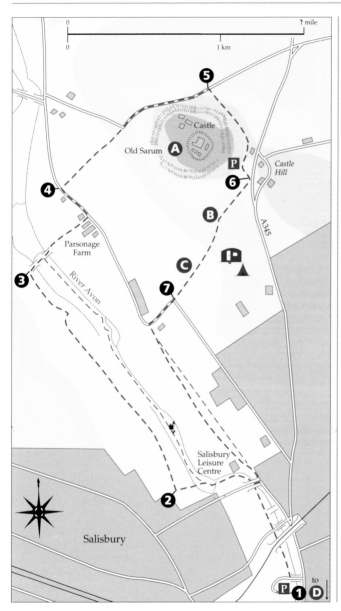

The route between Old and New Sarum (Salisbury) provides a delightful riverside walk and a chance to follow the footsteps of the Roman legions along Ackling Dyke. This walk can be combined with Walk 12.

Old Sarum was Hardy's 'Old Melchester'. In his day it was heavily overgrown and swarmed with rabbits. Its deep ditch was filled with trees. There are still trees on the slopes of Old Sarum, but English Heritage keep the grass mown around its fascinating ruins, notably the outline of the old cathedral. The bishop was responsible for moving the cathedral and town to a new site 2 miles (3.2 km) to the south, to what we know today as Salisbury.

Route description

1 Start from Salisbury's main car park, which is signposted from Castle Street. Walk back to the river and walk away from the town centre with the river on your right. Continue under road and rail bridges, with the river still on your right. When you reach a children's playground on your left, bear away from the river.

2 Cross a field to a gap at the end of a hedge, with allotments on your left. This footpath is the legal right of way. A popular unofficial alternative is to continue along the bank of the river, but although there are stiles over the fences, there may be muddy patches in wet weather.

3 When you reach a public footpath signpost to Devizes Road (on your left) turn right to cross the Avon by a footbridge. Go ahead to a road. Turn left at Old Sarum View.

4 Turn right up a farm track. Maintain your direction when you reach a road at its bend.

5 Turn right along the fenced track, and bear right to visit Old Sarum. Continue along the path, through another gate and down towards the main road.

6 Just before the road, turn right along the signposted footpath, with the hedge on your right. Fork left along the hedged track at the end of the first field. Ignore a stile on your right before the Parliament Tree stone.

7 Go straight on at the corner of a road to a signposted footpath on your left as the road bends right. Cross the stile to a fenced path. Continue past houses and bear right on to a gravelled path. At the end of the path, turn right on to a cycle path. At the end turn right and cross the river by a footbridge. Turn left to retrace your steps to the car park.

Points of interest

A Old Sarum was originally an Iron Age hillfort. It remained in continuous habitation, however, with Romans, Saxons, Danes and Normans living behind its ramparts and earthworks. William the Conqueror inspected his victorious army here in 1070. His nephew, Bishop Osmund (later St Osmund), built a castle and a cathedral, but just five days after the cathedral's consecration in 1078 it was struck by lightning and largely destroyed. The nave survived to be incorporated into Bishop Roger's restored cathedral. It remained an unhappy site for such an ecclesiastical building, however. Roger had also built a castle which was to serve as the bishop's palace, but the proximity of the civil and religious authorities led to antagonism. A lack of water was a problem and gave the clergy an excuse to move to a home of their own. The wind was bitterly criticised, while it was claimed that 'the whiteness of the chalk causes blindness'. No one disputed Bishop Poore when he said that a vision of the Blessed Virgin told him to build at a certain place which local people would direct him to. This proved to be the site of the present Salisbury cathedral, 2 miles (3.2 km) to the south in the unpromising wetland near the river. Work on building the new cathedral started in 1220 and the bishop moved to New Sarum in 1226. The body of St Osmund was removed to a shrine within the new building. To King Alfred the Great is attributed the saying 'there is nothing in that which men say, to wit, that a thing happens by chance'. Considering the history of the removal of Old Sarum's cathedral to modern Salisbury, how strange it is to discover that both sites are on one of the classic examples of a ley line. An alignment was first noticed by Sir Norman Lockyer and Alfred Watkins quoted it in *The Old Straight Track* (published 1925). Later researchers, notably Paul Devereux, have marginally changed the ley's angle and confirmed an 18 mile (29 km) alignment which starts at a tumulus north of Stonehenge, strikes the edge of the earthwork of Stonehenge just where it meets the Avenue (leys often strike the edges of earthworks rather than going through their centres) and continues to Old Sarum. There is a fine view of it running south from the ruins of the Norman Castle towards Salisbury Cathedral, where the ley passes just to the east of the spire and on to the north-west corner of the earthworks of Clearbury Ring. It continues south of this wooded Iron Age camp to Frankenbury Camp, east of Fordingbridge.

Until the Reform Bill of 1832 Old Sarum was one of the 'rotten boroughs' because it returned two MPs to Parliament with an electorate of only ten people. One of those MPs was William Pitt the Elder, who became Prime Minister.

B Old Sarum was the Sorviodunum of the Romans. This path is on the line of Ackling Dyke, the Roman road from Exeter via Dorchester and Badbury Rings. It met other Roman roads from Winchester, Silchester and the Mendips at Old Sarum.

C Near this spot beneath the spreading branches of an elm tree the Members of Parliament for the Borough of Old Sarum were, in former times, elected. The most notable MP for the Borough of Old Sarum was William Pitt, afterwards Earl of Chatham. This borough was abolished in 1832.

D The excellent Salisbury and South Wiltshire Museum houses a model of Old Sarum, clearly showing the conical hill, protected by an outer wall and ditch. It also shows the buildings that once stood there. The museum is in the beautiful setting of Salisbury Cathedral Close. It is housed in the King's House (where Richard III slept). This used to form part of the college where Sue (in *Jude the Obscure*) and Hardy's sisters trained to be teachers. The museum is open Monday to Saturday, 10.00 to 17.00 (Sundays in July and August, 14.00 to 17.00).

Walk 12
SALISBURY

3 miles (4.8 km)   Easy

Salisbury is a delightful city which was built in the 13th century when it was decided to move the cathedral and town of Old Sarum to a new site. This walk takes you through the city centre to see the magnificent cathedral and other buildings of interest. It also takes you along stretches of the River Avon and the River Nadder. This walk can be combined with Walk 11.

Salisbury is Hardy's 'Melchester'. It was 'a quiet and soothing place, almost wholly ecclesiastical in its tone; a spot where worldly learning and intellectual smartness had no establishment'.

Route description

1 Start from Salisbury's main car park (charge), which is signposted off Castle Street. Walk back to the river and follow the River Walk signs towards the city centre with the river on your left, and the cathedral spire ahead.

2 Turn left to the Church of St Thomas Becket. Follow the lane on the left of the church. Turn left into St Thomas Square and then right into Blue Boar Row.

3 Turn right across the Market Square and walk along Ox Row. Turn left in the corner to the Poultry Cross. Turn right into Silver Street, then left down High Street. Pass under an arch towards the cathedral.

4 Turn right to Mompesson House, then left down West Walk past the Regimental Museum and the Salisbury and South Wiltshire Museum.

5 Turn left towards the west door of the cathedral, then bear right along Broad Walk to go through an arched gateway (closed from 22.00 to 07.30) on your left to De Vaux Place.

6 Turn right to follow the Avon Valley Path sign to cross the Avon and bear right up Harnham Road, passing the Rose and Crown Hotel on your right. Continue past All Saints Church on your right.

7 Fork right down Lower Street. Turn right at the Three Crowns Pub along the Town Path. Pass the Old Mill Hotel on your left as you cross the Nadder. Constable painted his famous picture of the cathedral from the Town Path. Continue across fields.

8 Cross a footbridge to Queen Elizabeth Gardens. Bear right across a second footbridge and turn left to Crane Bridge Road. Turn right and then turn left after the bridge to walk with the Avon on your left.

9 Cross the road to enter the Maltings and walk with the river now on your right back to the car park.

Points of interest

A St Thomas Becket's Church was the scene of Sue's wedding to Phillotson in *Jude the Obscure*. The Doom Painting over the Chancel Arch is the largest in England. It was painted around 1475 as a thanks-offering for a safely-returned pilgrim.

B The Poultry Cross in Silver Street dates from the 15th century.

C Mompesson House is one of the finest Queen Anne town houses in Cathedral Close. It was built for a rich merchant at the start of the 18th century and is renowned for its elegant plaster-work ceilings and superb oak staircase. It also contains fine period furniture and the important Turnbull collection of 18th-century English drinking glasses. It has an attractive walled garden which is enclosed on one side by the great wall of the Cathedral Close. The house is in the care of the National Trust and is open daily (except Thursday and Friday) from March to October.

D The Duke of Edinburgh's Royal Regiment Museum ('The Wardrobe') houses an excellent military museum, a fine medieval house and a large riverside garden. The original house was built in 1254, and in the 14th century the Bishop used it as a store for his clothes and documents (hence 'The Wardrobe'). Open April to October, Sunday to Friday, 10.00-16.30 (daily in July and August).

E The excellent Salisbury and South Wiltshire Museum is in the beautiful setting of Salisbury Cathedral Close. It is housed in the King's House (where Richard III slept). This used to form part of the college where Sue (in *Jude the Obscure*) and Hardy's sisters trained to be teachers. The museum is open Monday to Saturday, 10.00 to 17.00 (Sundays in July and August, 14.00 to 17.00).

F The Norman cathedral was at what is now Old Sarum, but at the start of the 13th century the See was moved to New Sarum (Salisbury). Salisbury Cathedral is the only medieval cathedral in England to be built throughout in the same early English style. It was started in 1220 and completed in 1258. The impressive west front is just as it was in the 13th century. The spire was added later and soars to 404 ft – the tallest in England. Its treasures include one of the three originals of Magna Carta and England's oldest working clock. In the 14th century Edward III built a wall around the cathedral, and much of this wall surrounding the close survives. The close is entered through medieval gateways, and many of the buildings within it date from the Middle Ages. The 13th-century chapter house and cloisters lie to the south of the cathedral. Hardy called Salisbury Cathedral 'the most graceful architectural pile in England'.

G Harnham Mill dates from 1135. In 1550 it was Wiltshire's first paper mill, when the river was diverted from its present course under the building.

Walk 13
BREAMORE MIZMAZE

5 miles (8 km)   Easy

This is a peaceful walk on the edge of the New Forest. The route is along clear tracks across farmland and through woodland. The walk's chief asset is a rare maze hidden in the woods.

If you rely on public transport, start the walk at Breamore House. This is signposted from Breamore, which is on the route of the X3 bus between Poole and Salisbury. This will add an extra mile (1.6 km) to the walk.

Route description

1 Start from the village of Whitsbury, which is on a minor road 4 miles (6.4 km) north-west of Fordingbridge. Park your car in the village, perhaps near the Cartwheel Inn.

Walk up the main street, away from Fordingbridge towards Whitsbury Manor House and stud farm.

2 Do not turn right at the sign to Whitsbury Manor Stud, but do turn right 30 yards (27 m) later at the

signposted bridleway, where the road bends left. Follow this surfaced track, with the manor house and its stables on your right. Bend right behind the stables with this track before forking left along a signposted bridleway.

3 At the bottom of the hill, go ahead across a track to go over a stile beside a gate. Keep straight on with the hedge on your right to reach woodland. Continue over cross-tracks to walk out of the wood and up a field, with the fence on your right to a stile beside a gate.

4 Turn right along this track. Look for a half-hidden sign on the edge of the woods on your right. This will point out the way to the Mizmaze, which is hidden in the woods. Bear right to see it. Return to the track and bear left between two hedges. Fork right to follow the path through woodland.

5 Pass Breamore House on your left. Follow the driveway to a gateway guarded by stone lions. Turn left to visit the church. Retrace your steps to cross over the drive. Continue on to pass the Countryside and Carriage Museum on your left. When you reach the corner of a road, turn right. Pass the thatched cottages of Upper Street and turn right at a grassy triangle. This road leads to a hedged track.

6 Ignore a left fork and go ahead to a stile beside a gate. Continue with the hedge on your left to a gate. Turn right along a track.

7 When this track starts to bend right, turn left through a gate towards a stud farm. Go ahead through the yard and walk up a tree-lined track to woods. Turn right at the far side of these woods to a house with lamp posts. Turn left along the fenced track. At its end, bear left, then right, to reach Whitsbury Church. Go through the gate opposite the church door to follow a fenced path back to the village of Whitsbury.

Points of interest

A If it weren't for the trees that have overgrown the ditch beside this bridleway, you would have a fine view of Whitsbury Iron Age camp. It is surrounded by a triple circle of great banks with two deep ditches in between them. A circular timber house of 25 feet (7.5 m) diameter was excavated inside it in 1960, and Iron Age pottery found. The camp formed a link in the defensive chain which held up the Saxon advance into this area of Britain until the late 6th century. The Romans sank a 300 feet (90 m) well near the camp's western entrance. Finds of 2nd-century coins suggest that a Romano-British village existed at Whitsbury. Whitsbury probably derived its name from the colour of its chalky soil. Alfred Watkins, however, whose *Old Straight Track* was published in 1925, identified 'white' names with ancient salt tracks.

B Breamore Mizmaze is a curious medieval maze, ideally situated in a woodland clearing. This is a large maze with a diameter of 87 feet (26.5 m) and a low mound about 6 inches (0.15 m) high and 18 feet (5.4 m) in diameter at its centre. The Mizmaze is a labyrinth cut into the turf whose exact purpose and date of construction are unknown. The Labyrinth at Knossos, in Crete, was of a similar design. It has no false paths to lead you astray, just a single laborious route to the centre. A pattern soon emerges, with symmetry obviously important. The 'turn maze' could have been trodden as a significant ritual as long ago as the Bronze Age (1500 BC). Mazes, or 'Troy towns' (a name which may be a clue to their origin) used to be fairly common, but only eight in the whole of Britain seem to have

survived. Cromwell's puritan fanatics were responsible for destroying many of them.

C Breamore House is a fine Elizabethan manor house, built in 1583. The interior was damaged by fire in 1856 but has been restored. It has a fine collection of paintings and tapestries and is open to the public every afternoon from May to September, except Mondays and Fridays, and every day in August. Charge includes entry to the house and two museums.

D Breamore Parish Church is on the edge of the park close to Breamore House. It is Saxon but also displays Norman and later work. Over the archway to the south transept is an Anglo-Saxon inscription meaning 'Here the Covenant becomes manifest to thee'.

E You can also visit the Breamore Countryside Museum, which provides a fascinating insight into the days when village life was self-sufficient. There is a replica of a farm worker's cottage, a blacksmith's shop, a dairy, a brewery, a saddler's shop, cobbler's shed, village shop and school. The Breamore Carriage Museum is housed in the Queen Anne Stables adjoining Breamore House and contains a fine collection of horse-drawn vehicles and fire-fighting equipment.

F Upper Street contains some very well-preserved thatched cottages.

G St Leonard's Church, Whitsbury, dates from at least the 12th century, although the present building is mostly 19th century. William Hill restored and refurnished the church in 1963, emphasising the village's links with the world of horse-racing. St Leonard is the patron saint of prisoners.

Walk 14
BOKERLEY DYKE

4 miles (6.4 km)   Moderate

This is a walk through superb countryside with wonderful views over the New Forest. The walk follows the edge of Bokerley Dyke, a defensive earthwork that now forms part of the border between Dorset and Hampshire. It also takes you across downland into the village of Pentridge.

Pentridge was renamed 'Trantridge' by Hardy. Tess was a farm worker here, while Alec d'Urberville lived in Trantridge with his widowed mother. Tess walked the tracks from here to 'Chaseborough' (Cranborne) for some Saturday night fun at the fair. General Augustus Pitt-Rivers, who excavated Bokerley Dyke, was a friend of Hardy.

Route description

1 Park your car in the village of Pentridge and start the walk from the church. Pentridge is on the left as you travel along the A354 from Salisbury to Blandford Forum. Buses (nos. 184 and 185) from these places stop where the lane for Pentridge leaves the main road. With the church behind you, cross the village green to go through a small gate ahead. Continue with the hedge on your left to a gate which gives access to the road.

2 Turn left along the road until it turns left. Turn right at this corner to follow a green lane. Keep right when you reach a fork.

3 Continue ahead, ignoring a track which joins yours from the right. Follow the downland path to the great earthwork of Bokerley Dyke. This marks the boundary between Dorset and Hampshire. A few yards (metres) beyond the Nature Reserve notice turn right to walk on the Hampshire side of the Dyke. There are fine views over Hampshire and Wiltshire on your left, while the Dyke is on your right.

4 Turn right along the chalk track which cuts through the Dyke by the Nature Reserve board. After 100 yards (90 m) turn sharp right along the track waymarked with blue arrows. Turn left off this after another 100 yards (90 m) through a small gate waymarked with blue arrows. Walk with a fence on your right through trees to emerge overlooking the Dyke, going away on your right. Continue with the fence on your right until you reach the corner of a field.

5 The right of way bears left across this field to a prominent group of ash trees. You may find this path ploughed and obstructed by crops, although the farmer will also have probably left a clear headland path around the edge of the field which you should follow to the trees. Go through the gate behind the trees to walk with the hedge and views over the New Forest on your left.

Points of interest

A Where the path reaches the road, it crosses the course of the Dorset Cursus. This is a Neolithic (New Stone Age) earthwork running north-east from near Blandford Forum and is one of the largest prehistoric monuments in Britain. It consists of two parallel banks about 90 yards (82 m) apart and seems to have been a forerunner of the stone avenues such as those at Avebury. The number of barrows in this area has led to the suggestion that the Cursus could have been a processional way to them. Unfortunately, there is nothing to be seen here now as all trace of the Cursus has been ploughed out at this end. The best place to see this mysterious monument, which runs for 7 miles (11.2 km) across Cranborne Chase, is near Wyke Down, about 2 miles (3.2 km) south-west of Pentridge. Turn off the A354 along the B3081 for half a mile (0.8 km), where it crosses Ackling Dyke, the old Roman road. There is a right of way along this Roman road. Walk south along it for 1 mile (1.6 km) to where it crosses a well-preserved section of the Cursus.

B Notice a Neolithic long barrow in the field on your right. This is one of several long and round barrows in this area.

C Bokerley Dyke, or Ditch, is an impressive earthwork dividing the modern counties of Dorset, to the south, and Hampshire, to the north. It is not the result of any county boundary changes in 1974, however, as it dates from more warlike days when Britons clashed with Saxons at the end of the Roman occupation. Its origin is open to speculation because of the civil disturbances at this time. The Dyke has been accurately dated, however, with several stages of construction having been identified. Pitt-Rivers made his most celebrated excavation here between 1888 and 1891. He was able to show how the 4 mile (6.4 km) long Dyke plugged a gap beside the Roman road, Ackling Dyke, which connected Badbury Rings and Old Sarum. Its flanks were covered by forest. Initially, about AD 360, the road passed by the barrier. The Dyke was then extended across the road, blocking it. This may have been in 367 (coins of Valens, who was emperor from 364 to 378, were found). The Roman road was then re-opened, only to be blocked for good in about 395 (a coin of Honorius, dating from 393, was found). The Dyke's Hampshire side is more impressive and would have faced the Saxons. Its defenders on the Dorset side would have been the cultured Durotriges tribe. The Saxons were held at bay for about 150 years, well into the 6th century and long enough for Dorset to retain a Celtic character. Martin Down, on the Hampshire side of the Dyke, is a National Nature Reserve. Its unploughed sheep pasture supports chalkland butterflies, such as the silver-spotted skipper and the adonis blue. You may even see a ground-nesting stone curlew, but remember that it is an offence to deliberately approach or disturb this bird during the nesting season.

D The less impressive earthwork leading off at a right angle from Bokerley Dyke is known as Grim's Ditch. It is older than Bokerley Dyke and may have been constructed in the Bronze Age.

E Penbury Knowle is crowned by a simple single ditch Iron Age hillfort.

F Pentridge is a sleepy little village. The influence of Bokerley Dyke may have led to Pentridge church being dedicated to the Celtic Saint Rumbold. Look for a memorial on the north wall of the nave to the great-great-grandfather of the poet Robert Browning, also known as Robert Browning, who died in 1746. His son Thomas kept the Woodyates Inn which was well-known for its assocation with the Duke of Monmouth, whose Protestant rebellion of 1685 failed.

Walk 15
BADBURY RINGS

3 miles (4.8 km)   Easy

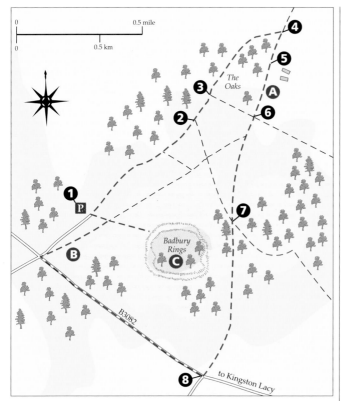

6 Go straight ahead as the track bends left past the signpost along a fenced path.

7 Go through trees into the next field. Ignore the track beside the trees on your left and go ahead with the hedge on your right.

8 Turn right along the road (or along the pleasant path parallel to it behind the roadside trees).

Points of interest

A This is Ackling Dyke, the Roman road from Dorchester to Old Sarum. It was intersected by a road from Poole Harbour to Bath just to the north-east of the Rings. This is probably the location of the Roman settlement of Vindocladia (White Ditches). The 'agger' or metalled surface of the Roman road stands 6 ft (1.8 m) high and is between 40 feet (12 m) and 50 feet (15 m) wide. Ackling Dyke was probably raised as early as AD 90 and was a great highway for 300 years.

B This is another stretch of Ackling Dyke.

C Badbury Rings is an excellent example of an Iron Age hillfort. It was built by the Veneti not long before the Roman invasion of Britain, and was designed for slingstone warfare. Some of the ditches are more than 60 feet (18 m) deep and may have been nearly twice as deep 2000 years ago. The outermost of its three concentric ramparts is nearly a mile in circumference, so a visit to the Rings can be a walk in itself. Despite achieving the peak of its builder's technology, Badbury Rings was one of the first forts captured by the Second Augustan Legion under Vespasian in either AD 43 or 44.

This walk takes you to the prehistoric fort of Badbury Rings. Apart from the ancient monument, this is an oasis of natural downland, having been restored to sheep grazing after scrub clearance carried out by the Prince's Trust in 1984. It is also a popular picnic venue, but you can escape the crowds by following the clear tracks from Badbury Rings.

Route description

1 Park in the car park to the left (west) of Badbury Rings, which is signposted on your right as you come along the B3082 4 miles (6.4 km) north-west of Wimborne. Walk away from the Rings along the track with the fence on your left.

2 Go ahead around a gate and through a belt of trees to walk along a fenced track.

3 Follow the track into an oak wood. Go straight ahead at the crossing of woodland tracks marked by a signpost and, ignoring cross paths, go to the end of the wood.

4 Turn right at the signpost along the track with the forest on your right. This is the course of Ackling Dyke, the Roman road.

5 Continue along the track past a farm on your left.

Walk 16
OLD HARRY

3 Bear right along the uphill track to the top of the ridge of Ballard Down, with its view of Poole Harbour on your right (and Swanage on your left). Go through a gate on your right to pass a trig point on your right and follow the ridge point.

4 Continue through a gate in the direction of the obelisk.

5 Turn right off the ridge track to go through a gate. Pass an old stone seat enscribed 'Rest and be thankful'. Continue down to Studland.

6 Go through a gate to continue along a lane, ignoring left turnings.

7 Cross a road to walk up to the church. Go ahead through the churchyard.

8 Turn right along the road back to the car park (turn left for the bus stop).

Points of interest

A Old Harry is the bigger and closer of the two rocks at the end of Handfast Point. It is also distinguished by its natural arch. The stump further out to sea is Old Harry's Wife. These are fine examples of coastal erosion. On a clear day you can see the Needles and the Isle of Wight from here.

B The two further chalk stumps off the shore walking south of Old Harry are known as the Pinnacles. A sea cave beneath the water between them is called Parson's Barn on account of its huge size. These are also textbook examples of coastal erosion.

C The Church of St Nicholas in Studland is almost entirely Norman. Grotesquely carved faces run along the north and south walls of the nave. Its chalice-shaped font dates from the 12th century, but the carved cross outside is modern, even showing the Concorde airliner.

This is a clear, waymarked walk offering fine views and excellent scenery. The walk takes you along the Dorset Coast Path from Studland Bay, past fascinating geological rock formations off the coast. The most prominent of these is the natural arch of Old Harry and the stump of his wife at Handfast Point. The Pinnacles and Parson's Barn cave are also impressive. The route then climbs up to the top of the ridge of Ballard Down, and then goes inland across fields to return to Studland.

The white cliffs between Handfast Point and Ballard Point (Hardy's 'Bollard Head') are described in *The Hand of Ethelberta*. In the final stages of this novel, Hardy writes of the steamer 'Spruce' avoiding 'a corner called Old-Harry Point, which lay about halfway along their track, and stood, with its detached posts and stumps of white rock; like a skeleton's lower jaw, grinning at British navigation'. Hardy and Emma lived in Swanage (the 'Knollsea' of Hardy's novels) soon after their marriage in 1875 and they must have walked these cliffs frequently.

Route description

1 Studland is at the end of the B3351, which leaves the A351 at Corfe Castle. A minor road (and no. 150 bus) connect it with Swanage and Sandbanks Ferry. Follow signs to South Beach Car Park, near Bankes Arms Hotel. Turn right from this car park along the road past the hotel until the road bends right.

2 Turn left to follow the blue arrows which mark the Dorset Coast Path to Old Harry. Follow this path, with the sea on your left, for 2 miles (3.2 km).

Walk 17
ST ALDHELM'S HEAD

5.5 miles (8.8 km)   Strenuous

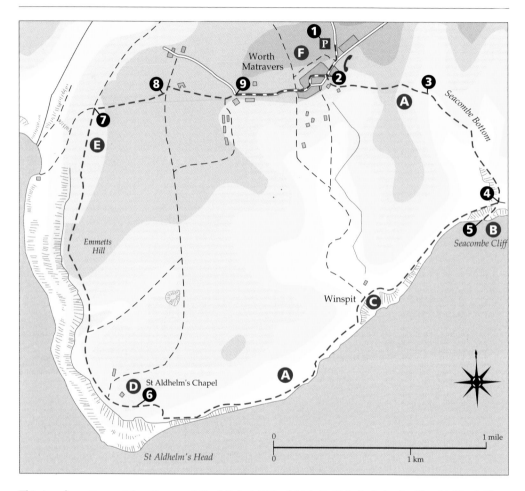

This is a dramatic coastal walk around the 360 feet (108 m) high St Aldhelm's (or St Alban's) Head. There are magnificent views of the Dorset coast; many of the rugged cliffs can only be seen from the coast path. The large cliffside quarries which provided Purbeck stone for London can be visited (**take great care at the quarries. DO NOT enter them**). Bats inhabit the unsafe caverns now. From the former quarrying village of Worth Matravers, the route follows a mixture of valley and coastal paths, and passes delightful places such as Winspit and Chapman's Pool. The coastline is superb and the Purbeck downland displays an abundance of wildlife including several species of blue butterflies. Puffins and orchids may also be seen on the walk. There are some steep ascents and descents on this walk.

Route description

1 Park at the car park (charge) on your right as you enter Worth Matravers from Corfe Castle. This is on a minor road off the B3069, which leaves the A351 (Poole–Swanage road) at Corfe Castle. Turn right from the car park towards the centre of the village, where there is a bus shelter (no. 144 bus between Poole and Swanage – not Sundays) near a duck pond.

2 Follow the road, which is a short cul-de-sac, opposite the bus shelter. Very soon you turn left up steps and along a waymarked path between gardens to a stile. Go ahead across a dry valley to a stile at the top of a hill and continue to another waymarked stile.   Bear right downhill to a signposted stile.

3 Follow the clear path on your right down this valley. Cross a plank to walk with the stream on your right and keep to the track down towards the sea. The path is now waymarked by small stone posts that mark the Dorset Coast Path.

4 Watch out for a stone post by a tree on your right. The route follows a steep path waymarked to Winspit. Before climbing this steep path, however, you can continue towards the sea, ignoring the waymarked Coast Path to Dancing Ledge on your left. Cross a stile to see the impressive limestone quarries and the cliffs at Seacombe.

5 Retrace your steps from Seacombe to turn left up the Dorset Coast Path towards Winspit, with the sea on your left. Follow the clear path along the cliffs to Winspit, where you descend bearing right, and go up the opposite side to bear left back to the cliff edge. Continue to St Aldhelm's Head, where there is a coastguard lookout and a 12th-century chapel.

6 Pass the coastguard's lookout on your left to continue along the cliff path. There are superb views from here over a series of cliffs and inlets. The view on your left from distant Portland via Lulworth and Kimmeridge to Chapman's Pool, ahead, compensates for the steep descent and climb up the opposite side of a valley. Cut steps and hand-rails here are a considerable help.

7 As you pass above Chapman's Pool, look for a stile in the wall on your right, near a Coast Path sign to Hill Bottom. Turn right, however, towards Renscombe. Go ahead to cross a second stile and continue towards a distant silage tower.

8 Bear slightly left to a stile in the wall ahead. Cross this stile and a track to a second stile opposite and continue in the direction of the silage tower. Cross two more stiles, with signposts, to reach a farm road. Turn left to reach a minor road.

9 Turn right along this road, passing the silage tower, to Worth Matravers. Fork left in the village to visit St Nicholas' Church and continue to the bus stop or car park.

Points of interest

A Notice strip lynchets at these places. These worn terraces are evidence of farming in the Middle Ages, when the land was ploughed in strips and steep banks were formed.

B **Seacombe quarries are too dangerous to enter** but are impressive enough from the outside. The Jurassic limestone from the disused cliff quarries here and at Winspit was used to build the public buildings of 17th-century London. The stone was mined here, carried on horn-carts pulled by men, then lowered by crane into waiting boats below. From Seacombe Cliff you can see as far as the lighthouse at Anvil Point, near Swanage.

C Winspit Bottom is a dry valley on whose slopes the terraces of medieval field systems (strip lynchets) are clearly visible. Winspit also had large quarries and produced stone until the 1940s. The old mines can be inspected from a distance but are not safe to enter.

D St Aldhelm's Head is named after the first Bishop of Sherborne, who was appointed in 705. There is a coastguard lookout, and a Norman chapel which, with its metre-thick walls, has solidly withstood the buffetings of storms for 800 years. The chapel was originally used by a priest who performed masses for the safety of sailors. Its headland location suggests it may also have been used as a navigation beacon for shipping. The use of radar was pioneered at St Aldhelm's Head in World War II. The term St Alban's is a misnomer but is commonly used in the local area.

E These stone benches and table were built by the Royal Marines to the memory of marines killed 1945–1990.

F Worth Matravers is a delightful village with quaint stone cottages, a fine Norman church and ancient farmsteads. It was once the reputed home of the notorious smuggler, Gulliver. The church at Worth Matravers is dedicated to St Nicholas, the patron saint of sailors. It has a beautiful chancel arch enriched with chevron moulding.

Walk 18
CORFE CASTLE

3.5 miles (5.6 km)   Moderate

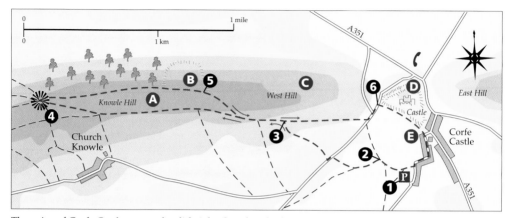

The ruins of Corfe Castle are a splendid sight. Standing high on a hill, the Castle guards the only gap in the Purbeck Hills, with mellowed stone cottages grouped in the village below. This walk takes you to Church Knowle and then along the ridge path to Corfe Castle itself.

Route description

1 Park in the car park (charge) signposted off West Street, Corfe Castle, which is on the A351 between Wareham (nearest British Rail station) and Swanage, and on the 142, 143 and 144 bus routes between Poole and Swanage. Look for a stile on your right from the car park and follow its yellow waymark arrow down to a footbridge over the River Corfe.

2 Cross the bridge and bear left to a stile beside a gate in the fence on your right. Go ahead with a ditch on your right before bearing right to a stile beside a gate giving access to a lane. Turn left and proceed for 30 yards (27 m), then turn right over a stile. Go ahead uphill to another stile in the fence ahead.

3 Turn left along the bridleway, waymarked with a blue arrow. Keep to this bottom track, with the hedge on your left through two gates passing the lime kiln on your right. Cross a stile and continue until a stile beside a gate on your left invites you to Church Knowle. Instead of going left to the church, however,

bear right uphill. Cross a stile and continue to the ridge.

4 At the commemorative stones, turn right along the ridge path. Go through a gate and walk with a fence on your right to a stile beside a gate ahead. Continue towards two round barrows ahead.

5 Follow the path beside the fence on your right to a gate. Bear right downhill to the bottom bridleway. Turn left along it, with a fence on your right, all the way to a gate leading to a lane. Turn left over a bridge.

6 Turn right along a footpath with Corfe Castle above on your left. Emerge near the castle entrance. Turn right past the Cross for West Street. Pass the entrance to the Model Village and continue to the car park.

Points of interest

A Church Knowle lime kiln was restored by the Ramblers' Association in 1988.

B A famous ley line runs through tumuli on Knowle Hill and the northern side of Corfe Castle. It strikes the southern side of the northernmost of the two tumuli.

C Here is another tumulus on the Corfe Castle ley line.

D The ruins of Corfe Castle are fundamentally Norman, but this was the site of a Saxon lodge where the scheming Elfrida had her step-son Edward the Martyr murdered in 978. The Saxons were punished for this crime with the rule of Elfrida's natural son, Ethelred the Unready. King John extended the castle in the early 13th century. Queen Elizabeth I gave it to Sir Christopher Hatton, a Lord Chancellor in the 16th century. Sir John Bankes, Attorney-General to King Charles I, purchased the castle eight years before the Civil War. This conflict brought Corfe Castle's finest hour, but resulted in it becoming one of the castles which Cromwell 'knocked about a bit'. The resolute Lady Bankes twice withstood sieges before her tiny garrison was forced to surrender in 1646. Open daily March to October (Sat and Sun in winter).

E The village to the south of Corfe Castle was the centre of Purbeck's stone and marble industry in the Middle Ages.

Walk 19
DURDLE DOOR

2.8 miles (4.5 km)   Moderate

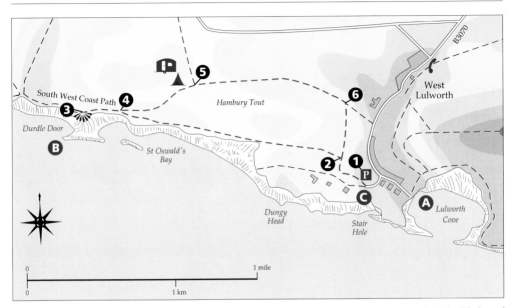

This walk follows a section of the Dorset Coast Path which includes Durdle Door, one of the highlights of this coastal walk. The views are tremendous, from Portland Bill in the west, to St Aldhelm's Head in the east. The return route is along downland paths.

Route description

1 Start from the car park at Lulworth Cove, which is also the bus stop for the Dorset Queen service no. 220 between Dorchester and Coombe Keynes (Wednesdays, Fridays and Saturdays only). Lulworth Cove is at the end of the B3070, 5 miles (8 km) south of Wool. Walk out of the car park, with Lulworth Cove behind you, along a clear, chalky, track.

2 Cross a stile beside a gate. Bear left along the track to the top of the cliff. This is the Dorset Coast Path, which you follow (with the sea on your left) for 1 mile (1.6 km) until you see the natural arch of Durdle Door, jutting out towards Portland across Weymouth Bay.

3 Retrace your steps past Durdle Door, now on your right, to a low waymark stone.

4 Fork left uphill along the path to the caravan site. A fence joins your path from the right. Ignore a stile in it, but go through a gate ahead.

5 Just before you reach the caravan site, turn right over a stile beside a gate. Bear left to walk beside the hedge on your left. Continue with the fence on your left, crossing two waymarked stiles.

6 Ignore a stile on your left which is signposted to West Lulworth Youth Hostel. Continue to Lulworth Cove car park. Then visit the Lulworth Cove Heritage Centre.

Points of interest

A Lulworth Cove can be seen as you rest or look back on your initial climb up the path to the cliff-top from the car park. It features in Hardy's writings as 'Lulwind Cove' and is where the dashing but ruthless Sergeant Troy is thought to have drowned in *Far from the Madding Crowd*.

B The natural rock archway of Durdle Door was formed by the sea wearing away the softer clays that join the promontory to the main cliff.

C Lulworth Cove Heritage Centre has permanent exhibitions on smuggling, paddle steamers and oil in Dorset. Open 10.00-18.00 Mon-Sun (October to Easter 11.00-16.00 Tue, Wed, Thur, Sat & Sun).

Walk 20
LAWRENCE OF ARABIA

6.3 miles (10.1 km)   Easy

Although this walk begins overlooking a military wasteland, don't be discouraged. Soon you pass T.E. Lawrence's ('Lawrence of Arabia') cottage at Clouds Hill. The walk then enters the forest, to emerge at Moreton, where Lawrence is buried. An Ordnance Survey map is recommended for this walk.

'Lawrence of Arabia' was one of Hardy's most valued friends. He often motorcycled to Max Gate to talk with Hardy, making his last visit in November 1926, before being posted to India. He finally settled on Hardy's 'Egdon Heath' because it reminded him of the desert.

Walk 20   LAWRENCE OF ARABIA

continued

Route description

1   Start from a car park on the east side of the road to Clouds Hill, nearly 1 mile (1.6 km) north of Bovington Camp.

Walk northwards (right) along the road to pass Lawrence of Arabia's Cottage on your right. Go straight ahead at a T-junction through dense undergrowth as directed by a blue arrow on the roadsign. Veer right across heathland to a track between 'Out of Bounds' notices and follow it. Cross over a wide track and cross back. Continue until a narrow path forks left from it to a road junction. Go ahead along the road opposite. When it reaches a triangle at a crossroads, turn left along a bridleway through the forest.

2   Keep straight ahead at a crosstracks and pass a pond on your left. Walk under power-lines and past conifers. Continue through broadleaved trees to reach a minor road.

3   Continue along the track ahead. Fork left into the wood, passing beehives. Go through the wood until you reach a T-junction. Turn right and carry on to a footbridge and bear right to a second, longer footbridge (over the River Frome). Go ahead to Moreton church and to Lawrence of Arabia's grave.

4   Retrace your steps past a signpost with yellow arrows, by a stile on your left.

5   A few yards (metres) further on turn right along the waymarked track. Fork left as waymarked and follow this track until a yellow arrow points up a track on your left. Turn left along this and fork right after 300 yards (270 m) along a waymarked path (look for a yellow dot on a tree). Bear left at the edge of the wood to follow the fence back to the road and the car park.

Points of interest

A   T.E. Lawrence's cottage is in the care of the National Trust and is open between April and September on Wednesdays, Thursdays, Fridays, Sundays and Bank Holiday Mondays from 14.00 to 17.00. It is also open between 13.00 and 16.00 on Sundays only from November to March. Lawrence first rented the cottage whilst serving as 'Private T.E. Shaw' in the Tank Corps at Bovington in 1925. He came here to get away from the camp and work on his 'Seven Pillars of Wisdom'. He wrote: 'I don't sleep here, but come out at 4.30pm till 9pm nearly every night, and dream, or write and write or read by the fire, or play Beethoven and Mozart to myself on the box.' His gramophone and typewriter are still here. There was no kitchen. Lawrence enjoyed picnics of 'stuffed olives, salted almonds and Heinz baked beans'. Lawrence later bought the cottage and settled here upon taking his discharge from the Services in 1935.

Lawrence was born at Tremadoc, Gwynedd, in 1888. He was the illegitimate son of Thomas Chapman and the Chapman family nursemaid, Sarah Maden. Unable to marry, his parents changed their names to Lawrence and settled in Oxford, where Thomas Edward was to read history at Jesus College, earning a first-class degree. He had studied the castles in Syria and returned there as an archaeologist.

When the First World War broke out he became an Intelligence Officer, based in Cairo. In 1916 the Arabs revolted against the Turks and the British offered an alliance. Sent to decide which of Grand Sherif Hussein's sons to support, Lawrence chose Feisal and rode with his warriors. His exploits were regarded as of 'inestimable value' by British High Command. His colleagues wrote of his 'gallantry' and his 'brains as well as dash'. He became ashamed of his vanity and for passing on promises that he knew the British would not keep. After the war he worked to see these promises kept. Feisal became King of Iraq and his brother Abdullah became King of Jordan. Although he despised drill and bull, Lawrence sought anonymity by joining the R.A.F. as J.H. Ross in 1922 and then as T.E. Shaw when entering the Royal Tank Corps. He was seen by others as the man to reorganise the R.A.F. in the run-up to the Second World War. On 13th May 1935, he was severely injured in an accident on his beloved motorcycle. He swerved to avoid two young cyclists as he was returning from Bovington. He died a few days later in Bovington Hospital and was buried at Moreton. After his death Churchill commented: 'I had hoped to see him quit his retirement and take a commanding part in facing the dangers which now threaten the country'. The Greek inscription over the door of his cottage means 'nothing matters'.

B   The cottage Hardy imagined as Clym and Eustacia's home in *The Return of the Native* still stands in the shade of tall Scots pines at Alderworth. Clym found his house 'almost as lonely as that of Eustacia's grandfather, but the fact that it stood near a heath was disguised by a belt of firs which almost enclosed the premises'.

C   St Nicholas' Church in Moreton was damaged when a German bomb fell in its churchyard in 1940. The replacement windows were engraved by Laurence Whistler in 1958.

D   T.E. Lawrence's grave is marked by a stone designed by his friend Eric Kennington, who also sculpted Hardy's statue in Dorchester.

E   Bovington Camp has been the home of the Royal Armoured Corps since the 1920s. The Bovington Tank Museum houses the largest collection of armoured fighting vehicles in the world. It is open daily all year, while the public can watch mock battles on the last Sunday in July.

Walk 21
BERE REGIS

5.5 miles (8.9 km)   Moderate

This walk crosses a stretch of Egdon Heath, unspoilt since Hardy's day, to reach the valley of the River Piddle or Puddle. Bere Regis is a watercress-growing village and the return to the village takes you past watercress beds where you may see a little diesel engine pulling trucks of watercress along a narrow gauge railway to the packing-shed. Woodbury Hill at the end of this walk is Hardy's 'Greenhill', where you can imagine the fair in *Far from the Madding Crowd*. The summit of this hill still retains an ancient earthwork 'in good preservation'.

The Saxon queen Elfrida retired to a nunnery at Bere Regis, remorseful after having her step-son Edward murdered at Corfe Castle in 979. Simon de Montfort, the founder of Parliament, also lived here for a while. It is the Tudor heritage that draws the tourists, however. Cardinal Morton lavishly decorated the church, while Henry VIII granted the manor of Bere Regis to Robert Turberville and with it the right of burial in part of the church. Hardy was to give a new twist to this family freehold when Bere Regis became 'Kingsbere' in *Tess of the d'Urbervilles*.

Route description

1 Follow the signs to the car park near Bere Regis church. Bere Regis is at the junction of the A35 and the A31 between Dorchester and Bournemouth (and on the 187, 188 and 189 bus routes between these towns). Visit the church, then bear left from its south porch to a gate leading to the road to Wool. Turn right to cross a bridge over watercress beds and turn right up Southbrook.

2 Ignore a stile on your right as the road bends left. When the road bends right proceed straight ahead up a footpath past a cemetery on your left. Continue between high hedges to a patch of woodland. Look for blue arrows painted on the trees and bear half-right uphill between two oak trees (the left one has an arrow painted on it). Go ahead along a clear path which veers right through bracken. Continue straight ahead at a cross-tracks to pass an old standing stone on your left before another path junction. Continue straight on downhill. Go through an old pollarded oakwood to a hedged track. Go through a gate and bear left as directed by a waymark to pass a farm on your right and reach a lane.

3 Turn left along this lane and continue for almost 1 mile (1.6 km). Bear left at a junction with a road to Bere Regis but turn right at the next road junction towards Wool. After 300 yards (270 m) you will come to a fork in the road. Don't go ahead along either fork, but turn left along Hollow Oak, a rough track.

4 Walk down to the watercress beds. Cross the narrow gauge railway and a footbridge. Follow the path to Dodding's Farm and turn left as directed by a yellow arrow just after a house on your left. Walk with a fence and the watercress beds on your left. Bear left over a stile into the next field and walk with the little railway on your left.

5 Aim for the church tower as the little railway veers left. Look for a waymarked stile in the fence ahead, near farm buildings on your right. Cross it and follow the path with the barn on your right. Bear left to reach the road to Wool again. Turn right towards Bere Regis. Pass the Royal Oak Hotel on your left and cross the road ahead to continue along North Street. Turn right down Blind Street to reach the A35 road. **Cross this**

carefully to go ahead along the way-marked hedged path opposite. Go through a gate and walk uphill with a hedge on your left. Maintain your direction across a track, over a stile, across a field and over another stile down to a lane. Look for another stile opposite and slightly to your right and walk uphill through trees. Cross a stile and bear slightly left to a gate.

Points of interest

A In the Middle Ages Bere Regis was famed for its fairs, and was a favourite resort of kings on their way to the south west. The Church of St John the Baptist, Bere Regis, is reputedly the most visited church in Dorset. It was fortunate to be spared when most of the village was destroyed by fire in 1788. Two iron hooks, dating from about 1600, hang either side of the church door. They were used to pull burning thatch off the roofs of cottages. The church roof is unique. It was a present from Cardinal Morton to his birthplace in 1425. He became Lord Chancellor of England, Archbishop of Canterbury and chief adviser to Henry VII. The author of 'Utopia', Thomas More (later Sir Thomas More), also grew up in his household.

The most striking features are the 12 figures (apostles?), dressed in Tudor costume, staring down at the congregation. Morton's mother was a member of the Turberville family. So was Jack Durbeyfield in Hardy's *Tess of the d'Urbervilles*. Tess's father, he was convinced that 'there's not a man in the county o' South Wessex that's got grander and nobler skillentons in his family than I'. The family 'skillentons' lie in the Turberville family vault under a beautiful square-arched Tudor window bearing the Turberville Crest, a 'castle argent', and their arms, 'a lion rampant'. These insignia also appear on a seal and a spoon in the possession of the Durbeyfield family. Tess

told Alec d'Urberville about them. When Tess's father dies and the family is evicted, Tess, her mother Joan and the six younger children, fill a hired wagon with all their worldly goods, including a large four-poster bed, and move to Kingsbere. Their promised lodgings are already let, however, so the bed is set up beneath the south wall of the church on land that is their freehold, being above the family vault. 'Over the tester of the bedstead was a beautifully traceried window, of many lights, its date being the 15th century. It was called the D'Urberville window'. Inside the church 'within the window under which the bedstead stood were the tombs of the family, covering in their dates several centuries. They were canopied, altar-shaped and plain: their carvings being defaced and broken; their brasses torn from the matrices. The rivet-holes remaining like martin-holes in a sand-cliff'.

Alec d'Urberville may have lain on the altar-tomb of Robert Turberville (Lord of the Manor from 1547 to 1559) under the east window when he pretended to be an effigy. Tess was deceived at first and she afterwards knelt by the large stone in the middle of the aisle (the entrance to the vault) to ask, 'Why am I the wrong side of this door?'.

B The standing stone on your left is known as the Devil's Stone.

C On Woodbury Hill, just east of Bere Regis, stand the remains of an Iron Age fortification. The views from here stretch as far as Poole. Woodbury Hill is Hardy's 'Greenhill'. Its flat plateau was the site of an annual sheep fair and Gabriel Oak brings Bathsheba's and Boldwood's flocks here: 'Men were shouting, dogs were barking. . . but the thronging travellers in so long a journey had grown nearly indifferent to such terrors, though they still bleated piteously'.

Walk 22
TOLPUDDLE

This walk explores the valley of the River Piddle, and the attractive heathy ridge to the south of it. Tolpuddle is a place made famous by its Martyrs, who suffered transportation to Australia in 1834 for daring to form a trade union and demand a wage increase.

Route description

1 Start from Tolpuddle village green, where the Martyrs used to meet under the old sycamore tree. If you can't park here, try the Martyrs' Inn. Tolpuddle is on the A35 between Puddletown and Bere Regis. It is served by bus nos. 186, 187 and 188. Walk away from the village green down the lane towards Southover.

2 Ignore a waymarked gate on your right, bend left with the lane and turn right. Bear left to pass a thatched cottage on your right and continue along a rough, hedged track. Keep to this track, ignoring all turnings until the track enters the wood ahead.

3 Turn right at the cross-tracks. Follow this track, ignoring all turnings, until a track cuts across from your left. Fork right downhill to walk with a field on your right. Bend left with the track to a gate.

4 Continue with the fence on your right and a fine view across the Frome valley on your left. Pass a conifer plantation on your right. Go ahead through a gate into an oak wood and follow the path near the fence on your left.

5 Turn left through a small gate and turn right immediately past a thatched cottage. Go through a gate and turn right through a way-marked gate to walk along the right-hand edge of a field to a gate into the wood. Follow the hollow way, ignoring cross-paths down to Athelhampton. Turn left along the A35. Athelhampton House is on your right. After visiting the house and gardens, retrace your steps along the main road. Turn left along a path behind the church.

6 At the end of this track, go ahead through a waymarked gate to walk with the hedge on your left. Continue through a waymarked gate (ensure it is shut to prevent cows getting at young trees) to go ahead along a track. When this track bends right go ahead through a waymarked gate. Proceed to a small gate in the far left-hand corner of this field and go straight ahead to a gate giving access to a lane. Continue along the lane until you reach the lane on your left leading back to Tolpuddle.

Points of interest

A   Whether you arrive in Tolpuddle by bus or car, you will soon see evidence of the Tolpuddle Martyrs. Near the bus stop at the Bere Regis end of the village can be seen a plaque on the wall of a cottage. This used to be Thomas Stanfield's cottage and the plaque reads:

'Dedicated by the Trades Union Congress to the memory of the six agricultural labourers of this village whose trade union meetings in this cottage led to their being sentenced to seven years' transportation in 1834.'

They had formed a (legal) Friendly Society of Agricultural Labourers in order 'to preserve ourselves, our wives, and our children from utter degradation and starvation'. They planned, by withholding their labour, to force farmers to increase their wages from eight shillings to ten shillings a week. If you park near the village green you will see the old sycamore tree under which the Martyrs met. A thatched memorial shelter now stands near it. An exhibi-

tion about the Martyrs is housed in one of the six Memorial Cottages at the Dorchester end of the village. They were erected by the Trades Union Congress in 1934 to mark the centenary of their martyrdom.

Also erected to mark their centenary, unveiled at precisely 4pm on 31st August 1934, was the headstone marking the grave of James Hammett, the only one of the Martyrs to return to Tolpuddle. He was buried in the churchyard in November 1891, having almost reached his 80th birthday. He died in Tolpuddle workhouse and his grave was unmarked for 42 years. This is the church that Owen Graye helped restore in Hardy's *Desperate Remedies*, and it really was restored in the mid-19th century, although the carved Purbeck marble coffin lid of Philip, a 12th-century priest, survives, as does the 14th-century roof. Hardy's Owen Graye stayed with his sister Cytherea in an old farmhouse nearby while the church was being restored. This farmhouse must have been the manor house.

At the other end of the village, beyond the bus stop, can be seen the memorial gateway at the Methodist chapel, where George Loveless (the leader of the Martyrs) was a lay preacher. James Loveless, George's brother, was another Martyr, as was Thomas Stanfield's son John. The sixth Martyr was James Brine, while James Hammett had been arrested in mistake for his brother John.

These were hard times in rural Dorset and the ruling class feared riots. They therefore had the six men arrested for administering secret oaths. Brought to trial in Dorchester in March 1834, they were sentenced to seven years' transportation to Australia. They were never violent.

A storm of protests and petitions to Parliament ensued the verdict. A massive trades union rally was held in London and the families of the

six, who had been refused parish relief by the magistrates and evicted from their cottages, were helped by a specially set up London Dorchester Committee. Pressure continued until two years after the trial. A threat to indict the king's brother, the Duke of York, for administering secret oaths as Grand Master of the Orange Order, led to the king granting the Tolpuddle Martyrs a free pardon. The news took a further two years to reach them (George Loveless read of his pardon in an old newspaper handed down by his master). They finally returned to great celebration in London. Money was raised to lease two farms for them in Essex, but after six years all except James Hammett emigrated with their families to Canada.

B   Athelhampton is a 15th-century mansion with 16th-century additions. It was damaged by fire in 1992 but most parts of the building remain on display to the public. Visit the Great Hall, Great Chamber, Wine Cellar and King's Room. The beautiful grounds contain eight walled gardens, fountains, pavilions and topiary pyramids. Open April to October, 12.00 to 17.00.

C   Ilsington House is a William and Mary mansion built by the 7th Earl of Huntingdon in 1690. It was regularly used by the Royal Family as the final overnight stop before Weymouth and it was the childhood home of George III's illegitimate grandson. It is situated in 6 acres of formal and landscaped gardens and contains a fine collection of period furniture and a varied private art collection. It is open May to September, on Wednesdays, Thursdays, Sundays and Bank Holidays, from 14.00 to 18.00.

D   Tolpuddle Martyrs Museum was built in 1934 by the T.U.C. in memory of the six agricultural workers who were transported to Australia in 1834. It is open Tuesday to Sunday, 09.00 to dusk. Free.

Walk 23
PUDDLETOWN

3.6 miles (8.8 km)   Easy

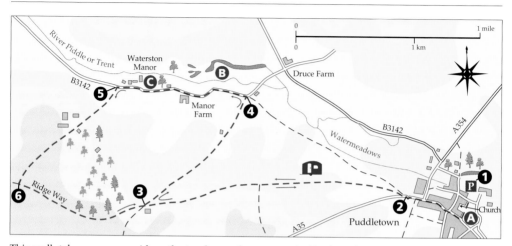

This walk takes you over wide paths to places where scenes in *Far from the Madding Crowd* were set and to places associated with its characters. Puddletown is the 'Weatherbury' of Hardy's novel. Hardy had relations in Puddletown, the Sparks family, and he often walked to visit them as a child, so he was able to draw on a rich store of memories.

Route description

1 Park your car near St Mary's Church, in the centre of Puddletown. This is a village at the junction of the A35 and the A354. The 184, 187, 188 and 189 buses connect it with Salisbury, Weymouth and Bournemouth. Take the footpath to the right of the church and turn right along the A35, past the school on your right.

2 Pass the bus stop at the end of the village and fork right up the wide, hedged bridleway which runs to the right of a Caravan Club site. Continue along this bridleway for over 1 mile (1.6 km), ignoring two turnings on your left.

3 Go through a gate ahead and turn sharply right along a bridleway down to the B3142 road.

4 Turn left along this road 100 yards (90 m) after passing Waterston Manor on your right.

5 Walk up the track, passing farm buildings on your right. At the end of the fenced track, turn right through a gate and bear left uphill.

6 Go through a gate ahead and turn left along the ridgeway back to Puddletown. Take care to bear right through the gate at the cross-tracks just before a corrugated iron hut.

Points of interest

A St Mary's Church is the centre of attraction, being the best example of a medieval church in Wessex. There is a 12th-century font, old high box pews and a musicians' gallery which was erected in 1635. Thomas Hardy's grandfather, when a young man in the late 18th

century, played the violoncello here. In 1927, the year before he died, Hardy brought his friend Gustav Holst here. Gabriel Oak, the shepherd in *Far from the Madding Crowd*, sang here. His employer, the woman farmer Bathsheba Everdene, didn't appreciate his sterling qualities until he told her he intended to emigrate. A box pew under the gallery has 'Henery' carved inside it, perhaps inspiring the spelling of Henery Fray, another of Bathsheba's employees.

B This meadow, where in May 'just now every flower that was not a buttercup was a daisy', was the setting of the sheep-washing scene in *Far from the Madding Crowd*.

C Waterston Manor was immortalised as Bathsheba's home.

Walk 24
EGDON HEATH

3 miles (4.8 km)   Moderate

This walk takes you along the forest track of Puddletown Forest. Hardy named this area Egdon. It is a collection of heaths between his home and Bournemouth, and this is its western edge, nearest his birthplace. The landscape of much of Egdon Heath has been radically transformed, being overpopulated in the east and afforested.

Route description

1 Park your car in the signposted car park on your right at the entrance to Puddletown Forest at Beacon Corner, where a minor road from Puddletown bends left. This is 1 mile (1.6 km) south-west of Puddletown, where the A354 joins the A35 and the 184, 187, 188 and 189 buses pass on their way to Salisbury, Weymouth and Bournemouth.
Walk back to the bend in the road and, facing the forest from the direction of Puddletown, go ahead westwards along the forest track.
2 Turn left uphill through pine trees. Ignore a path that joins yours from the left. Bear right at the next track junction.

3 Fork left. Ignore a downhill track on your left but turn immediately right along a green path. Emerge at a crossing point of five tracks and take the second from your left. Fork right only to bear left to a crossing point of six tracks.
4 Take the second track on your right. Ignore a yellow waymark as the track bends right. When this track bends right again, look for a yellow arrow waymarking a path through the trees ahead. Bear right along it down to the A35 road.
5 Turn right along a path beside the road for 200 yards (180 m). Go through a gate and follow the track into the forest. Ignore a track to your right and bear left. When the track bends right, bear left towards

the A35. Turn right along the old road, parallel to the A35.
6 Ignore the first track on the right, but turn right at the second. Ignore a green track coming in from the right and keep on ahead when a track joins yours from the right. Ignore a track from the left, but take the track on your left at the next crossing point back to the start.

Points of interest

A Hardy was fascinated by the heath's mysterious round hollows scooped out of the earth and evident here on both sides of the path. He had lain in one as a child, buried among the ferns 'reflecting on his experiences of the world so far as he had got'.
B This is the area where 'Mistover Knap', the home of Eustacia Vye, was located in *Return of the Native*. Unlike Eustacia, who wanted away to 'the great arteries of the world', Clym Yeobright enjoyed the smell of the heath as he cut furze. 'Bees hummed around his ears with an intimate air, and tugged at the heath and furze-flowers at his side in such numbers as to weigh them down to the sod. . . Tribes of emerald green grasshoppers leaped over his feet, falling awkwardly on their backs, heads or hips, like unskilful acrobats, as chance might rule; or engaged themselves in noisy flirtations under the fern-fronds with silent ones of homely hue.'
C The old road parallel to the modern A35 is where, beneath the overhanging trees, Hardy places the sad meeting between Troy and the weak and ill Fanny Robin, struggling to reach the workhouse in *Far from the Madding Crowd*.

47

Walk 25
HARDY'S COTTAGE

3.5 miles (5.6 km)   Easy

This is a walk through the true heart of Hardy's Wessex, where he was born, grew up and wrote two of his most famous novels – *Under the Greenwood Tree* (1872) and *Far from the Madding Crowd* (1874).

Route description

1 Start from the car park near Hardy's cottage. Coming from Dorchester, follow the A35 road towards Puddletown. After 3 miles (4.8 km), turn right along a lane to Higher Bockhampton. Turn left towards Hardy's cottage, but turn right after 100 yards (90 m) for the car park.

Follow the signposted woodland path to Hardy's cottage, bearing left uphill from the car park. Ignore a path on your right but continue to a signpost where you turn left, then bear right. Turn left down to Hardy's cottage.

2 Turn left around Hardy's cottage to walk down Bockhampton Lane. Pass the turn for the car park on your left and go ahead to the road (Cuckoo Lane). Turn left along it for 50 yards (45 m) then turn right up the waymarked, hedged track (Hardy's 'drong'). When it bears right, keep straight on through a gate into a field to walk with a hedge on your right. Notice the monument to Admiral Hardy straight ahead on the horizon.

3 Go through a waymarked gate and follow the well-trodden path straight ahead across the middle of the field to a track where you turn left to reach a minor road.

4 Cross the road and continue along the waymarked bridleway ahead. Keep the fence on your right until you go ahead through a gate to walk with the fence on your left. Bear left, whilst overlooking Kingston Maurward Manor on your right. Go through a gate to cross a field to a gate ahead on your left. Follow a track to a gate which gives access to a lane.

5 Turn right and bear right again. Follow the road as it bears left, keeping the Elizabethan manor house on your left. Go through a gate beside a cattle grid. Continue past the demonstration orchard and garden of the Dorset College of Agriculture on your left. Go through a small gate beside a cattle grid. Walk past the bungalows of Knapwater on your left to reach the old schoolhouse on your left.

6 Turn left to follow the road through Lower Bockhampton. Go ahead to a crossroads, where you turn right towards Tincleton. Turn left after half a mile (0.8 km) along the track to Pine Lodge Farm.

7 Pass Pine Lodge Farm on your left and go ahead through two waymarked gates. Walk with the hedge on your left to the wood ahead, where you turn left along a path around its edge. Descend to a gap in an iron fence and bear left along a track. Pass waymark no. 10 but bear right when you reach picnic tables. Pass waymark no. 4 to reach the car park.

Points of interest

A Thomas Hardy was born in this cottage on 2nd June 1840. You can view the interior, including the bedroom where Hardy was born, by prior appointment only. Telephone Dorchester (0305) 62366 or write,

with an SAE, to Hardy's Birthplace, Higher Bockhampton, Dorchester, Dorset DT2 8QJ. You can see the front exterior and garden without an appointment between 11.00 and 18.00 (or sunset) from April to October (except Thursdays). Hardy's Birthplace is a National Trust property, but it is also the home of its tenants, who act as custodians. On your way in, notice the squint window in the porch where Hardy's grandfather used to watch for Excisemen coming to search for smuggled spirits. The sound of a whiplash on the bedroom window-pane in the early hours of the morning would see Hardy's grand-father going downstairs to bring in tubs of brandy left on the threshold. He would hide these safely away until the smugglers returned to collect them. Hardy's grandmother told young Thomas old tales at the (now restored) great inglenook fire-place. Hardy's grandfather built the cottage in 1800 and in the poem *Domicilium* Hardy recalls his grand-mother's account of the place when she first settled there. This was written by the teenage Hardy after his grandmother's death in 1857:

'Our house stood quite alone, and those tall firs, And beeches were not planted. Snakes and efts, Swarmed in the summer days, and nightly bats, Would fly about our bedrooms. Heathcroppers, Lived on the hills, and were our only friends; So wild it was when first we settled here.'

You can also see Hardy's room (shared with his brother Henry). Here he wrote *Under the Greenwood Tree*, in which Hardy's cottage is depicted as the home of Tranter Dewy. 'It was a long low cottage with a hipped roof of thatch, having dormer windows breaking up into the eaves, a chimney standing in the middle of the ridge and another at each end'. On the left is the stone-flagged room with its ceiling bisect-

ed by a low beam from which mistletoe hung for the Dewys' Christmas party. Hardy also wrote *Far from the Madding Crowd* here. Today, honeysuckle clambers up the walls and apple trees are scattered on the lawn, as when Hardy was a boy.

B The view of Admiral Hardy's monument must have interested his namesake. Hardy introduced his remote ancestor into his historical novel *The Trumpet Major*.

C Kingston Maurward House is an extravagant manor built close to an older one between 1717 and 1720 by George Pitt, who married Lora Grey, the last heiress of a longstanding local family. It is encased in dressed Portland stone because George II regretted it was 'built of b-b-brick'. The owner went bankrupt to please the King. In real life, Julia Augusta Martin lived here. She founded the village school (Hardy was its first pupil) and took a maternal interest in the young Hardy.

D The old manor house dates from the late 16th century.

E The old schoolhouse in Lower Bockhampton (Hardy's 'Lower Mellstock') is where Hardy spent his first year at school at the age of seven. He then went to school in Dorchester. Fancy Day was the teacher here in *Under the Greenwood Tree*. On the night of carol singing, young Dick Dewey goes missing and is found leaning against a tree gazing at Fancy's window.

F Thornecombe Wood and Black Heath together form a 66 acre (26.4 hectare) nature reserve. Look for a ridge crossing your path in Thornecombe Wood. This is the course of Ackling Dyke, the Roman road from Durnovaria (Dorchester) to Londinium (London) via Badbury Rings and Old Sarum. The ghost of a Roman centurion has been seen here, his feet elevated to the road's former height.

Walk 26
MAX GATE

5.5 miles (8.9 km)   Easy

This is a walk rich in associations with Hardy. Max Gate, the home that Hardy designed for himself, is passed on the walk, as is Stinsford churchyard, the last resting-place of his heart. The grave of Hardy's great friend William Barnes is visited, while many of the paths followed can be identified in novel, poem or biography. This is also the western end of Hardy's 'Valley of the Great Dairies' where Tess had her happiest days in *Tess of the d'Urbervilles*. After walking out with her Angel in these lush watermeadows, Tess marries him in the church that is passed at West Stafford.

Route description

1 Park your car at the end of South Court Avenue, which is reached from Maumbury Road in the south of Dorchester. Walk eastwards past St Mary's School on your left. Veer left through a new housing estate, turn right in Armada Way, then left to follow the road to reach the A352 at a roundabout. Turn right to cross a bridge over a by-pass. Before a second roundabout, cross the road to Max Gate on your left. Go past Max Gate and turn left up Syward Road to see the door in the wall on your left. Retrace your steps to the A352, and re-cross it at the roundabout ahead.

2 Go ahead along the footpath to the wood on the horizon, following the hedge on your left. Pass a stile

50

on your left and continue uphill. Go through a gap in the hedge and follow a well-marked path across the next field. Enter the wood through a gateway. Go on downhill to reach a lane. Cross it to follow the track opposite. When it bends right, look for a path to Winterborne Came Church on your right. Retrace your steps to the lane and turn right along it to reach the A352. Turn right towards Wareham.

3 Look for a lane on your left just before the A352 bears left. Follow the bridleway to West Stafford through a gate. Walk with the hedge on your left to a little gate ahead. Continue with the hedge on your right and the course of the Winterborne (winter stream) on your left.

4 Go through a gate ahead and pass gates in the hedge on your right to reach a gate in the corner of the field. Bear right beside the hedge to a gate and cross a road. Follow a track through a gate on your right. This leads under the railway. Continue along a track, ignoring a stile into a housing estate on your right. Turn right past the old rectory to St Andrew's Church, West Stafford. Turn left along the road just before the church. Cross a bridge over a branch of the River Frome and bear left to a road junction.

5 Turn right along the lane signposted 'Hardy's Cottage'. Just before the bridge to Lower Bockhampton, turn left along the path beside a branch of the River Frome. You come to a bridge over a tributary stream. (Note this bridge, as you will return to it.)

6 Fork right after the bridge to follow the path to Stinsford church. Walk round to the far side of the church to see where Hardy's heart is buried, opposite the seat.

7 Retrace your steps to the bridge mentioned at no. **5**, cross it and turn right. Go ahead over a footbridge and follow the wide path to a stile beside a gate. Follow a track under a

road bridge and turn left over a brick bridge to cross the River Frome.

8 Turn right at a road, then up the first road on your left. Keep ahead up a path when this road bears right and cross the railway by a bridge. Go ahead to the A352. **Cross this carefully** and turn right to reach a roundabout. Turn left through the housing estate to retrace your steps to St Mary's School and the start in South Court Avenue.

Points of interest

A The red-brick Victorian house of Max Gate belongs to the National Trust and is rented as a private residence. Visitors can view the garden and drawing room on Sundays, Mondays and Wednesdays, from March to September. Telephone (0985) 847777 for opening times. Although the house was designed by Hardy and was his home from 1885 until 1928, it no longer contains any of his memorabilia. Hardy died here on 11th January 1928. In 1886, Hardy wrote: 'Our life here is lonely and cottage like'. Here he wrote *The Woodlanders*, *Tess of the d'Urbervilles* and much of his poetry. Max Gate proved to be a magnet for his admirers during Hardy's lifetime and the garden door in Sywards Road was Hardy's escape route when he wanted to walk his dog 'Wessex' but avoid the crowds gathering at the front gate. The rich and famous also came here to visit Hardy, including the Prince of Wales and Lawrence of Arabia.

B Hardy's great friend and mentor was William Barnes, the Dorset dialect poet. Barnes left teaching to become the rector at both Whitcombe and Winterborne Came in 1862. Over 20 years later, Hardy was to visit him and talk 'of old families'. This was when Hardy had *Tess of the d'Urbervilles* in mind. William Barnes is buried at the foot of the Celtic cross in the corner of the churchyard. The 13th-century

church is dedicated to St Peter at Winterborne Came.

C St Andrew's Church, West Stafford, has been identified as the scene of Tess's marriage to Angel Clare in *Tess of the d'Urbervilles*. The three bells of 'Talbothays parish church' were rung for her wedding. One of this church's three bells dates from 1595 and the other two from 1620.

D Stafford House is best seen from the lane leading to Hardy's Cottage. Look right just after crossing the first bridge.

E This delightful riverside path is the 'embowered path' in *Under the Greenwood Tree*. Hardy's poem *The Dead Quire* tells how phantom singers passed this way to the church at Christmas and disappeared into the churchyard.

F Hardy's grandfather, father and uncle were all in the church choir of St Michael's Church, Stinsford. Immortalised by Hardy in *Under the Greenwood Tree* as the 'Mellstock Quire', the choir was replaced by an organ about the time of Hardy's birth. The musicians' gallery was probably removed about 1880. The porch of the church contains a sketch-plan by Hardy showing the shape of the gallery and where each player and singer sat. In the poem *A Church Romance* (subtitled *Mellstock: circa 1835*), Hardy wrote of his mother seeing her future husband in the gallery and falling in love at first sight: 'turned in the high pew, until her sight, Swept the west gallery, and caught its row, Of music-men with viol, book and bow.'

Hardy's heart is buried in the grave of his first wife, Emma. His ashes were interred at Poets' Corner in Westminster Abbey. Hardy wrote *Rain on a Grave* after the death of Emma: 'Soon will be growing, Green blades from her mound. And daisies be showing, Like stars on the ground. Till she form part of them – Ay – the sweet heart of them.'

Walk 27
DORCHESTER

3 miles (4.8 km)   Easy

3 Turn left and cross London Road, passing Town Bridge on your right. Continue along the path with the river on your right, passing the Exhibition Hotel on your left. Pass River Crescent on your left to go ahead up Mill Street. Turn right over the old bridge opposite the Swan Inn and turn right up Holloway Road.

4 Turn left up Pound Lane and turn left at the top to St George's Church. Bear right around the Green to South Walks Road, where you turn right up the track opposite no. 29. Go ahead in the shade of an avenue of chestnuts past a playing-field on your right. Continue down the tarmac path, then down Salisbury Terrace, then Salisbury Street, bearing left to Town Bridge. Turn left up High East Street.

5 Turn right into North Square with St Peter's Church on your left. Turn left up Colliton Street and left again down Grey School Passage, passing Trinity Church on your left.

6 Turn left down High West Street, passing the Dorset County Museum and the statue of the Dorset poet and friend of Hardy, William Barnes, on your left. Turn right down South Street (pedestrianised). Bear right at the road junction to Weymouth Avenue.

7 Walk down Weymouth Avenue as far as Maumbury Rings on your left. After visiting this ancient earthwork, walk to the road junction and turn sharply right up Maumbury Road. Immediately after the traffic lights, turn right down a footpath and turn left up West Walks. Keep straight on, passing the old Roman wall on your right, to the roundabout. Turn left, then right for the Top o' Town car park.

This walk takes you round Dorchester and as there is so much to see it deserves a full day. Dorchester is a very interesting town in its own right. Its history goes back to the Stone, Bronze and Iron Ages. The Romans established 'Durnovaria' in AD 70 as the tribal capital of the Durotriges. It was a Saxon centre in the 10th century. It was then taken by the Normans and used as a hunting centre by King John. Fires in the 17th and 18th centuries destroyed many of its medieval buildings and most of the buildings today are of Portland stone.

Dorchester is the capital of Hardy's Wessex and is the town in Wessex most associated with him. It is his 'Casterbridge' where *The Mayor of Casterbridge* was set.

Route description

1 Start from the car park at the crossroads known as Top o' Town in Dorchester. The entrance to the car park is on the junction of the B3150 (which joins the A35 towards Bridport) and the B3147 (which joins the A37 towards Yeovil). Walk back to the crossroads and notice Hardy's statue across The Grove (the road to Yeovil) on the left of the roundabout. Go ahead down High West Street.

2 Turn left up Glyde Path Road (also named Shire Hall Lane). When this road bears left, go straight ahead down steps. Pass the thatched 'Hangman's Cottage' on your left, cross the River Frome and turn right along the path beside the river.

52

Points of interest

A Hardy's memorial statue was sculpted by Eric Kennington. The grass and plants at Hardy's feet symbolise his beloved Egdon Heath. The statue is sited at the start of The Grove, one of Dorchester's avenues or 'walks'. Hardy wrote of 'the ancient defence of the town, planted as a promenade'. Along this walk Henchard tried to persuade Farfrae to remain in Casterbridge in *The Mayor of Casterbridge*.

B High West Street was described by Hardy as 'Timber houses with overhanging storeys, whose small-paned lattices were screened by divinity curtains on a draw string, and under whose barge boards old colonels waved in the breeze'. The Old Tea House, dated 1635, which you pass on your left at the top of the street, still fits that bill. The Old Crown Court was the scene of the trial of the Tolpuddle Martyrs who were sentenced to seven years' transportation to Australia after forming the trade union movement. The court is now a memorial to the Martyrs.

C Shire Hall is on your right when you turn down Glyde Path Road or Shire Hall Lane. This is where the Tolpuddle Martyrs (see Walk 22) were tried in 1834. The court was bought by the Trades Union Congress in 1955 and is preserved as a memorial to the Martyrs. Hardy wrote *The Mayor of Casterbridge* in a house, now demolished, in Shire Hall Lane.

D The Hangman's Cottage is a 16th-century thatched building close to the River Frome. It was formerly the home of the notorious Jack Ketch, the man who hanged the Duke of Monmouth's defeated supporters after Judge Jeffreys had sentenced them. It is now a private residence and features in Hardy's short story *The Withered Arm*.

E The path beside the River Frome divides town and country, as Hardy remarked: 'Casterbridge. . . was a place deposited in the block upon a cornfield. There was no suburb in the modern sense. . . reapers at work among the sheaves nodded to acquaintances standing on the pavement corner.'

F In Hardy's day, the Town Bridge was built of brick and attracted down-and-outs who accosted passers-by.

G Mill Street was Hardy's Mixen Lane, which consisted 'of thatched and mud walled houses by the sallows. . . the hiding place of those who were in distress and in debt and trouble of every kind'.

H Hardy liked to visit the old church of St George as he was a friend of the rector's sons. Later, whilst living at Max Gate, he attended services here. The church was built on a Roman cemetery and a first-century Roman tombstone inscribed to the memory of Carinus is preserved on the inner wall of the tower. There is also a Norman tympanum above the south doorway showing St George slaying the Turks at the Battle of Antioch. Hardy made Elizabeth-Jane meet Lucetta in this churchyard in *The Mayor of Casterbridge*, while nearby, either on Fordington Green (in front of the church) or on the playing-field which you pass before Salisbury Terrace, a rough gallows was erected in *The Dynasts*. An effigy of Napoleon was hung from it and set on fire by lighting a pile of wood below it. The flames lit up the 'grey tower of Durnover Church' (St George's Church) and when they reached the heart – an animal's bladder filled with gunpowder – the whole effigy exploded.

I The King's Arms was 'the chief hotel in Casterbridge'. Susan Henchard and her daughter Elizabeth-Jane looked through its window to see the husband who had sold her many years before. He was now Mayor of Casterbridge attending 'a great public dinner of the gentle-people and such like leading folk'.

J Trinity churchyard was overlooked by the seed shop that housed Henchard's last business in Casterbridge.

K The excellent Dorset County Museum in High West Street includes many treasures of Dorset. It is a delight for geologists, archaeologists and lovers of natural history. It is in fact run by the Dorset Natural History and Archaeological Society. There are also displays on Dorset rural life and a Thomas Hardy Memorial Collection which includes a reconstruction of Hardy's study at Max Gate. It is open Monday to Saturday, 10.00-17.00. There is an admission charge.

L The gossips used to meet near the town pump at the top of South Street. Gabriel Oak dressed in a shepherd's smock for the Candlemas hiring fair here in *Far from the Madding Crowd*. The Antelope Hotel is where Lucetta met Henchard in *The Mayor of Casterbridge*.

M A tall brick house on your left, now a branch of Barclay's Bank, was the model for Henchard's house. High on your right, opposite the Hardye Arcade (named after the founder of the grammar school), is a plaque to show where Hardy trained as an architect in Hick's office.

N Maumbury Rings, south of the town, was built by Stone Age Men as a Sacred Circle but was adapted by the Romans to form a vast amphitheatre where 10,000 spectators could watch gladiatorial combats. Its 'dismal privacy' was used for secret meetings in *The Mayor of Casterbridge*.

O Henchard found a home for his rediscovered wife and daughter about halfway along West Walks.

Walk 28
MAIDEN CASTLE

2 miles (3.2 km)   Easy

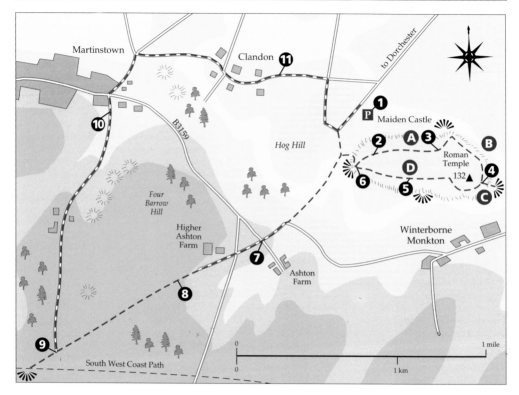

This walk is through a page of the unwritten history of Wessex. It takes you to Maiden Castle, one of the greatest Iron Age hillforts in Britain. The impressive earthworks of the Castle are easily accessible. It has triple banks and ditches enclosing 45 acres (18 hectares). It was at its peak in the final century before the Roman invasion, when it was the chief settlement of the Durotriges, the tribe which held Dorset. They were prosperous, with wheat production then rivalling yields attained in the Second World War. About 5000 of them lived in this hillfort. Excavators have found traces of their huts and numerous grain storage pits. Their defences were the peak of Iron Age technology, perhaps earning the hillfort its 'maiden' label for impregnability. Their chief weapon was the sling, and an ammunition stockpile totalling 54,000 pebbles from Chesil Beach has been found. Their wealth tempted the Roman Imperialists, however, who fired ballistae at the defenders and locked shields above their heads to reach the gates, which they smashed with battering-rams. Once inside, an indiscriminate slaughter of the inhabitants ensued. In AD 70 the new town of Durnovaria (Dorchester) was built nearby and peace returned to this hillside.

Finds from the site can be seen in the excellent Dorset County Museum in High West Street, Dorchester. The museum is run by the Dorset Natural History and Archaeological Society and is a delight for geologists, archaeologists and lovers of natural history. The museum is open Monday to Saturday, 10.00-17.00.

Hardy called the hillfort 'MaiDun'. From its 'huge dimensions and many ramparts', Henchard, 'glass in hand', often watched his step-daughter and Farfrae out walking in *The Mayor of Casterbridge*. From here he also saw the return of Newson. It is the scene of the story *A Tryst at an Ancient Earthwork*, unsurpassed as an evocation of place and mood. 'It may be likened', wrote Hardy, 'to an enormous many-limbed organism of an antidiluvian time, lying lifeless, and covered with a thin green cloth, which hides its substance, while revealing its contours'.

Route description

1 Start from the car park at Maiden Castle, which is signposted from the A354 on the southern outskirts of Dorchester. Walk along the track to enter the hillfort by the Western Entrance through a maze of banks and ditches.

2 Go ahead from the gateway across the interior, bearing slightly left to reach a hollow which once contained a dew pond.

3 Cross the bank barrow ahead and veer slightly left to see the remains of a Romano-British temple. Continue along the top rampart, with its excellent view over Dorchester on your left.

4 Inspect the double gateways at the eastern entrance to the hillfort. Continue along the southern ramparts.

5 Pass a circular hollow thought to mark a well on your right, with the southern ramparts on your left. Continue along these ramparts.

6 Turn left through the Western Entrance. Bear right passing tin huts on your right. Go through a gate below you on your right. Turn left and follow the track downhill. Go through a gate on to a lane and turn right.

7 Go straight ahead at a crossroads and left at a T-junction. Take the first lane on your right to Higher Ashton Farm. Go through the farm to a waymarked gate. Cross a stile and go through the yard to another gate.

8 Bear right up a field and turn right through a gate at the end of a hedge. Turn left through a waymarked gate. Go ahead, then through another waymarked gate. Continue across the next field, bearing to the left of the tumuli. Go through a waymarked gate in the top left-hand corner of the field.

9 Turn left and walk to the brow of the hill for an amazing view of the coast and Portland Bill and, to your right, Hardy's Monument. Retrace your steps and follow the farm track down past a farm. Continue down a lane.

10 Bear right past thatched cottages and cross a bridge over a stream. Cross a road and continue. On a right-hand bend turn up a track before a black fence on your right. Follow the track, passing a tumulus on your right. Go through a farm to reach a lane. Turn right, then left, to walk with farm buildings on your left.

11 When the lane bends left go straight on through a gate and along a fenced track. Turn right at crosstracks and continue uphill along another fenced track. Go through two gates to rejoin the path back to the car park.

Points of interest

A Maiden Castle is certainly the best-known hillfort in England. Here you cross the ditch and bank of an earlier, simpler earthwork that enclosed just 10 acres (4 hectares) at the eastern end of Maiden Castle.

B This Romano-British temple dates from about AD 370.

C The most dramatic moment in Maiden Castle's history came shortly after the Roman invasion of AD 43. The Second Augusta legion, commanded by Vespasian (who became emperor in AD 69), captured the hillfort. Excavations by Sir Mortimer Wheeler in the 1930s uncovered evidence of a fierce battle in AD 69 at the east gate, where elaborate outworks had been added in 20 BC.

D The separate ramparts have a relationship of distance and height to each other that was carefully calculated and engineered.

Walk 29
WHITE HORSE HILL

4.5 miles (7.2 km)   Moderate

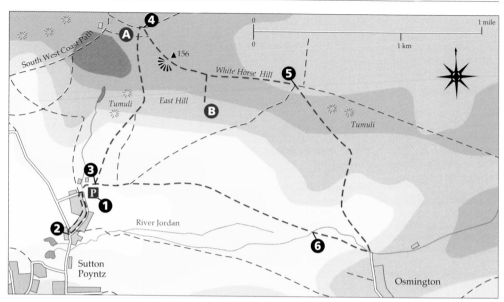

This walk takes you up on to White Horse Hill to see the chalk carving of King George III on his white horse, moving away from his favourite resort of Weymouth.

Route description

1 Park your car near the mill-pond at Sutton Poyntz. On the A353 from Weymouth to Preston turn left at the Ship Inn, then fork right to the Springhead Inn. There is an infrequent bus service from Weymouth to here and a frequent bus service (A) between Weymouth and Preston. Cross the bridge upstream of the pond and turn left to pass the pond on your left. Continue along the park beside the stream to the mill.

2 Turn left over the footbridge and go along the lane between the mill and the millhouse. Turn left around the mill and walk past the pond again towards the downs ahead. Turn right along the signposted path and turn left through Hunt's Timber Yard.

3 Cross a stile to go ahead across the field to a kissing-gate in its far right-hand corner. Bear slightly right uphill to a gate and follow the path which bears slightly left to the top of the down.

4 Turn right through a waymarked gate. Ignore a gate on your left beside a signpost and walk with a fence on your left and a fine view of Portland on your right. Divert right from the path immediately after the next gate to see the white horse carved on the hillside. Return to your path to walk with a hedge on your left along the top of the field to a gate ahead.

5 Bear right along the track downhill to the village of Osmington. Return to the footpath, on your left as you come from the village, where the road and houses end. Turn left through the gate towards Sutton Poyntz. The hedge is on your left and a stream on your right, with the White Horse on the hillside behind. Cross the stream in the corner of the field and bear right through a gate into the next field, with the White Horse ahead.

6 Bear slightly right across the field to bar stiles. Continue to a gate and across the corner of a field to another gate. Keep the hedge on your left as you go through another gate. Go through a second gate to a lane leading back to the start.

Points of interest

A Anne Garland watched the review of the troops from here.

B The White Horse covers more than an acre.

Walk 30
PORTLAND

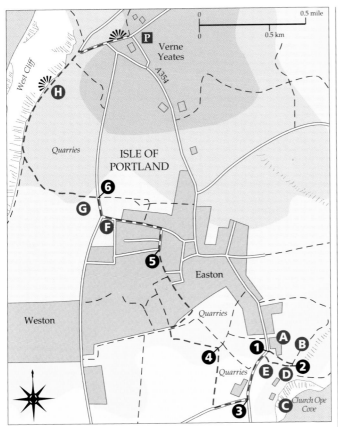

hedge on your left. Pass an old quarry on your right.

4 Turn left along the track to an old windmill. Fork right to a second old windmill. Bear right, then turn left beside the line of a dismantled railway. Pass a school on your left. Cross a road to continue along a path ahead which reaches the corner of a road at a footpath signpost.

5 Turn left along the third road on your left (the main road through the village of Reforne). Pass the George Inn on your left to reach St George's Church at the head of the road. Turn right along Wide Street for 150 yards (135 m).

6 Turn left along a signposted footpath. Bear right towards the cliffs. When you reach the road at a sharp bend bear right to reach the bus stop or car park near the war memorial.

Points of interest

A Portland Museum houses the Island's Shipwreck and Smuggling story. It is housed in Avice's Cottage, a 17th-century building featured in Hardy's novel *The Well Beloved*.

B In *The Well Beloved*, Jocelyn Pierston often 'paced down the lane to the Red King's Castle'.

C Church Ope Cove is the only natural landing-place on the island.

D Jocelyn sealed his engagement to the first Avice in *The Well Beloved* with a kiss among the ruins of St Andrew's Church.

E Pennsylvania Castle is Hardy's 'Sylvania Castle', which Jocelyn rented to be near Avice.

F The George Inn was where the 'Court Leet' (local council) met.

G Jocelyn first saw the second Avice in the churchyard of St George's 'where the island fathers lay'.

H Jocelyn walked here with Marcia.

The Isle of Portland is not really an island, since it is connected to the mainland by Chesil Beach. This is not a circular walk, but a frequent bus service from Weymouth to Portland stops at either end of the route. The Isle of Portland was Hardy's 'Isle of Slingers'.

Route description

1 Park near the war memorial or take one of the frequent buses from Weymouth to Portland Museum. From the museum bus stop, go down Church Ope Road which becomes a footpath which passes Rufus Castle on your right. Go down steps towards the beach. When the steps turn left, turn right along a narrow, hedged path signposted to a 13th-century church.

2 Go up steps past the ruins of St Andrew's Church. Turn right under an old arch and continue through trees. Pass Pennsylvania Castle on your left. Turn left along the road.

3 Turn right along Weston Street for 250 yards (225 m). Turn right along a signposted footpath, with a

Walk 31
MOONFLEET

4 miles (6.4 km)   Easy

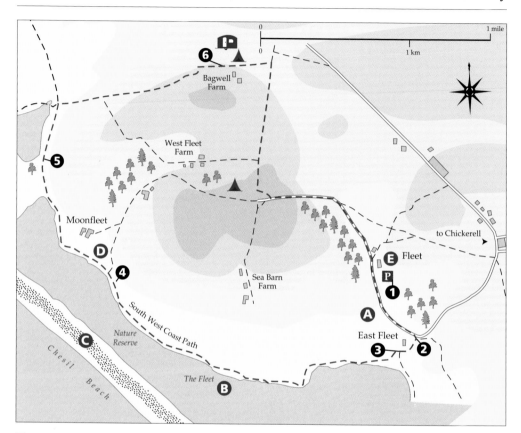

This is a walk of special interest to children, since it explores the setting of a children's classic: *Moonfleet*, by John Meade Falkner. The route takes you along a coastal path beside Chesil Beach and the Fleet Lagoon to Moonfleet, where you can descend to the beach at Gore Cove. Chesil Beach and the Fleet Lagoon are important areas for their wildlife. The Fleet Lagoon is the second oldest nature reserve in the country and has been protected for its mute swans, which are in abundance at the Abbotsbury Swannery (Walk 32). Many sea birds breed on the beach.

Moonfleet is a tale of smuggling on this coast involving the local Mohun family. Thomas Hardy's own grandfather was involved in the smuggling business, which was a common activity in these parts, especially with the increase of excise duties. Meade Falkner had plenty of facts to base his story on. The collector of Customs at Weymouth reported in 1717: 'Tidewaiter Edward Thorne and two assistants arrived near Fleet in the early hours to investigate a reported landing on the Chesil Beach. They were met by thirty men in disguise armed with clubs and other weapons who drove them from the place'. Sixty-nine men and women from along the Fleet were imprisoned at Dorchester between 1800 and 1821 for evading customs, including Joseph and Thomas Zealy from Fleet itself.

Route description

1 Park your car at Holy Trinity Church, Fleet. This church is on your right as you drive along the lane to Fleet from the B3157 at Chickerell, a north-western suburb of Weymouth, well-served by town buses. If you come by bus, walk down the lane from Chickerell towards Fleet, but start the walk at no. **2** instead of turning right for the church. If you drive to the church, walk back down the lane to the corner where it turns left.

2 From Fleet Church, turn right along the signposted path to Old Fleet Church. If you have walked from the bus stop at Chickerell, go straight ahead, passing cottages on your right, then go through a gate on your right to visit the old church. Return to the path and continue over a waymarked stile beside a gate. Bear right around the churchyard wall to a footpath signpost where you bear left towards Langton Herring.

3 Ignore a stile (signposted to Weymouth) on your left but cross a stile beside a gate on your right to walk with the Fleet Lagoon and Chesil Beach on your left. Continue over a stile and a footbridge along a narrow hedged path to a second field. Walk along this coastal path until you reach a footpath signpost.

4 Ignore a stile on your right and bear left along a hedged path. Continue across a footbridge and cross the field ahead, bearing slightly right towards Moonfleet Hotel. Walk with the fence on your left to a stile and Coast Path signpost. Pass a noticeboard about the Fleet Sanctuary on your left. Descend to the beach at Gore Cove.

5 Veer right to cross a signposted stile and walk with the wall on your right to another Coast Path signpost. Leave the Coast Path here by turning right over a stile, then immediately right for a few paces to turn left over a stile. Follow this signposted footpath with the hedge on your left.

Reach a stile in the corner of the field and go ahead with the hedge on your left to another stile.

6 Enter a campsite and keep the hedge on your left until the path turns left to leave the hedge on your right and the site shop on your left. Walk past a playground on your right to a stile in the fence ahead. Turn right along a track which bears left to a lane. Turn left down this lane back to the car park or bus stop.

Points of interest

A Just a few cottages remain of the original hamlet of East Fleet, since it was virtually destroyed by a terrible storm on 23rd November 1824. An eye-witness reported that 'the sea began to break over the beach at 5am. The water came up as fast as a horse could gallop . . . The nave of the church was undermined and demolished, also a cottage hard by and another at the end of Butter Street. Two cottages near the garden of the old Priest's house were also thrown down. Two old ladies living in the Priest's house were rescued from a bedroom window. A hayrick was swept away and seven large fishing boats were washed far inland'. The chancel of the old church was spared. Beneath it is the Mohun family vault with the old smugglers' secret passage. A brass plaque on the south wall commemorates John Meade Falkner. The Mohun family are also remembered here with two fine brass plaques. Robert Mohun acquired Fleet in 1566. His son, Maximilian, probably rebuilt the church to incorporate the family vault. The Mohuns were royalists who had their estate confiscated in the Civil War, although it was returned to them at the Restoration. They remained loyal to the Stuarts even when William of Orange landed. Robert Mohun (born 1715) was the last male heir, and Fleet passed, by marriage, to the Gould family. The heir to their fortune in 1818 was the bachelor Reverend George Gould, who was Rector of Fleet when the great storm destroyed his church. *The Sherborne Mercury* wrote: 'The Reverend George Gould, Rector of Fleet, a village destroyed by the late storm, intends building a new village: and with a degree of philanthropy that will ever immortalise his name, has taken and provided for all the sufferers under his roof.' *Moonfleet* was published a year after the Gould family line died in 1897.

B The Fleet is a lagoon between the mainland and Chesil Beach. It is a shallow stretch of water containing a lot of weed. Eels, bass and mullet abound, but may only be fished by a few locals. The Fleet has been a protected reserve since the 14th century. The east end of the Fleet is salty and tidal, but it becomes brackish and still in the west.

C The Dorset coastline here is dominated by Chesil Beach, a barrier of pebbles connecting the Isle of Portland with the mainland. It is over 17 miles (27 km) long and the stones increase in size towards the east. The stones come from as far away as Cornwall and have been mixed up by the tides. However, the stones are graded in progression of size. Some, near Portland, are as big as saucers, while they are considerably smaller near Abbotsbury. It is a fine example of the eastward drift of materials that occurs all along the south coast. The Isle of Portland acts as a huge groyne to prevent the pebbles moving on. Chesil Beach acts as a reef protecting the coastline behind it from erosion.

D Part of the Moonfleet Hotel was the Mohun family manor house.

E Fleet's new church was built between 1827 and 1829 at the vicar's expense. The apsidal chancel has a good vaulted plaster roof, and contains a large marble monument with mourning figures. It contains the old church bell.

Walk 32
ABBOTSBURY SWANNERY

2.5 miles (4 km)   Moderate

Abbotsbury is set in rolling countryside between the downs and Chesil Beach. Its unspoilt thatched cottages made it the ideal location for scenes in the film of Hardy's *Far from the Madding Crowd*. The famous Swannery is open from April to October and on Sundays in winter.

Route description

1 Park your car in the car park signposted on your left as you enter Abbotsbury on the B3157 from Weymouth. There are infrequent buses to Abbotsbury from Weymouth and Bridport (nos. 60, 201 and 210), and from Dorchester (no. 61). Leave the car park by the walled track towards the church.

2 Turn left through a kissing-gate into the churchyard. Turn right to pass the church on your left. Turn left around the church and fork right to a small gate. Continue through a gap in the fence to see the remains of Abbotsbury Abbey. Go ahead to the old millpond and turn right to a lane.

3 Turn right up this lane (Church Street) to the village. Bear left up Market Street.

4 Turn left up Chapel Lane, a rough waymarked track, towards the chapel on the hill ahead. Where Chapel Lane bends right, go ahead through a kissing-gate and bear right past farm buildings on your right. Continue uphill through a kissing-gate ahead.

5 Visit the chapel, cross a stile and bear left to the right-hand edge of a coppice. Cross a stile signposted 'Swannery', then descend to a stile in the hedge at the foot of the hill. Go on across a stile in the next hedge and over the chapel withy bed. Turn right to the Swannery.

6 Walk back past the withy bed to the Swannery car park. Follow the track on your left, signposted 'Coastal Path', past the old mill. Continue to the millpond and retrace your steps to the car park.

Points of interest

A Notice two medieval stone coffins in the churchyard opposite the porch of St Nicholas' Church. The porch contains the carved effigy of an abbot dating from about 1200.

B South of the churchyard gate is the Pynion End, the best part of the abbey remains. This wall dates from about 1400 and incorporates a fireplace.

C St Catherine's Chapel was retained as a landmark for sailors after the dissolution. It is built entirely of stone, roof and all, with heavy buttresses and thick walls.

D The withy bed is where willow is grown to be pollarded annually when the 6 ft (1.8 m) stems are used to tie up reed bundles.

E The Swannery was established by the monks in the 14th century. About 600 mute swans breed here.

F The building with a millstone against its wall was the abbey mill.

G The tithe barn is the largest in Britain. Built by the abbey in the 14th century, it is now used as a store for thatching reeds from the Fleet.

Walk 33
THE HARDY MONUMENT

3.5 miles (5.6 km)   Moderate

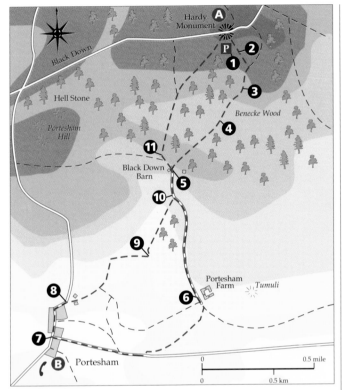

The monument on this walk is to 'the other Hardy', Sir Thomas Masterman Hardy, Nelson's flag captain at Trafalgar. He was born at Portesham in 1769.

Route description

1 Park your car below the Hardy Monument, which is by the road between Martinstown and Portesham. If you travel by bus (60 or 210 from Weymouth or Bridport), start this walk at Portesham. With your back to the monument and the sea in front of you, bear left along a distinct path through the heather down to conifers.

2 Descend through the trees to a level path. Turn right along this. Look for a blue arrow waymark where you fork left to a forest track.

3 This track bears right uphill. Look for a path through the trees on your left just before the track bears left. Follow the path to rejoin the track.

4 Stick to the waymarked track, ignoring a path which forks right. Go ahead at a cross-tracks at the edge of the forest to descend to a signpost.

5 Turn left and go through a gate uphill with a fence on your left. Pass

a gate and trees on your right and go ahead through a gate. Continue with a fence on your left and a wall on your right.

6 Pass a farm on your left, go through a gate ahead to follow a track which bends right downhill to a road. Turn right to reach Portesham.

7 Your way is on the right, up the road signposted to Hardy's Monument. First, however, visit Portesham church on your left. Bear right past Portesham Stores.

8 Fork right along the bridleway signposted 'Hardy Monument 1½'. Go along a hedged track to a gate then keep to the left side of a field. Follow the distinct track as it swings right.

9 Turn left along the walled track at the top of the field. Bear right to a gate and continue with the wall on your right to a gate in the corner of the field.

10 Turn left along the track you followed on your outward journey. This time, however, fork left at the bottom gate to a second signpost.

11 Bear right along the uphill path through the trees, ignoring tracks on your right until a right fork is signposted 'Hardy Monument ¼'. Go ahead to the monument and car park.

Points of interest

A The Hardy Monument was erected between 1844 and 1846 (Admiral Hardy died in 1839) and is an ugly octagonal tower over 70 ft (21 m) high. The view from here is magnificent. On your extreme right is Start Point on the south Devon coast, while the Needles can be seen on your extreme left.

B Read the interesting epitaph on the outside of St Peter's Church, Portesham, which refers to the Civil War.

Walk 34
THE DORSETSHIRE GAP

2.5 miles (4 km)   Moderate

This is a walk along the great chalk ridge that overlooks Blackmoor Vale. The walk is well off the beaten track. Park your car on the verge near Folly, where Walk 35 also begins. Look out for wild flowers and foxes.

Blackmoor Vale, the 'Vale of Little Dairies', is where Tess was born. 'The secret of Blackmoor', Hardy wrote in *Tess of the d'Urbervilles*, 'was best discovered from the heights around'.

Route description

1 Park at the roadside north of Folly, which is between Piddletrenthide and Mappowder about 10 miles (16 km) north-west of Dorchester. Walk eastwards along a track which crosses the road, passing a farmhouse on your right.

2 Ignore a greener track which forks to the right (and is followed in Walk 35). When your track turns right, keep straight on uphill with woodland on your left and a fence on your right. Bear left through a gate and turn right immediately along the hedged path.

3 When the hedge finishes on your left, turn left and walk towards a prominent water-tank. Continue across the field to a small gate in the hedge ahead. Veer slightly right downhill to a gate which leads to a

sunken track through woodland. Follow this track which gradually bears right.

4 When a similar sunken track comes in to meet yours from the left, turn left along it to a path junction. This is the famous Dorsetshire Gap. You won't appreciate it until you climb the slope on your left.

5 Having enjoyed the view, return to the foot of the slope and turn left along the path into the woodland signposted Armswell Farm, with steep banks on your left. Go ahead through a gate and continue with trees behind a fence on your left uphill to a gate in the hedge ahead.

6 Keep straight on with the woodland on your left. Go through a double gate. Pass farm buildings on your right and turn right through a gate, then turn left immediately to

follow a fenced track down to the road.

7 Turn left along the road back towards Folly and your car.

Points of interest

A Nettlecombe Tout is a fine lookout with a single ancient ditch. The earthwork seems to have been left uncompleted. Tout was a Celtic god, Romanised to Toutates. It was around here that Tess was compelled to look for work the winter following her desertion by Angel Clare. When Tess came to these uplands, the heights seemed friendly at first: 'In the middle distance ahead of her she could see the summits of Bulbarrow and of Nettlecombe Tout. . . They had a low and unassuming aspect from this upland, though as approached on the other side from Blackmoor in her childhood they were as lofty bastions against the sky'.

B The Dorsetshire Gap is a quirk of geology, where many steep slopes meet in a small area, as if a giant had folded the chalk like a pocket handkerchief. The view from the top of the slopes is breathtaking. Hardy described it in *Tess of the d'Urbervilles* '. . . the hills are open, the sun blazes down upon the fields so large as to give an unenclosed character to the landscape, the lanes are white, the hedges low and plashed, the atmosphere colourless. . . in the valley, the world seems to be constructed upon a smaller and more delicate scale; the fields are mere paddocks. . . Arable lands are few and limited; with but slight exceptions the prospect is a broad rich mass of grass and trees, mantling minor trills and dales within the major. Such is the Vale of Blackmoor'.

62

Walk 35
PLUSH

4.5 miles (7.2 km)   Moderate

The views on this walk are superb, especially those of Blackmoor Vale. The chalk hills form an amphitheatre around Plush, making this a quiet, remote place.

Route description

1 Park at the roadside north of Folly, which is between Piddletrenthide and Mappowder, about 10 miles (16 km) north-west of Dorchester. Walk eastwards along the track which crosses the road, passing a farmhouse on your right.

2 Fork right up a greener track to the gate. Bear right to the top of the down. Pass trees on your left and bear right beside the fence on your left, behind which is an Ordnance Survey pillar. Go ahead through a gate in the corner of the field, turn left through a small gate and immediately turn right.

3 Walk with the fence on your right to a gate on your right near a concrete reservoir. Turn right to follow the path down to a bar stile.

Cross it and veer slightly right downhill.

4 Go through a gate to descend to the bottom right-hand corner of this field. Go through a gateway and turn left along the road through Plush.

5 Turn right up the gated bridleway signposted 'Alton Pancras 1¼'. Bear right through trees and go uphill beside a hedge on your right. Continue through a gate and past trees on your right to go through another gate.

6 Go ahead along the downland path for half a mile (0.8 km). Bear left at a cement post marked 'FP'. Turn right to walk with the hedge on your left. Go through a gateway. Veer right and follow the hedge on your left. Pass a square earthwork

and dew pond on your right. Continue to a gate in the corner between two clumps of woodland. Bear right to follow the path through trees to a sign which points to Folly. Bear left over a stile and continue with a hedge on your left to return to Folly.

Points of interest

A This pillar is a trig point or triangulation station set up by the Ordnance Survey.

B Plush is the model for Hardy's village of 'Flintcombe-Ash' in *Tess of the D'Urbervilles*.

C Hardy's imaginary 'Flintcombe-Ash Farm' was situated on the slopes of Church Hill.

D This square earthwork has not been dated.

Walk 36
CERNE ABBAS

3.5 miles (5.6 km)   Moderate

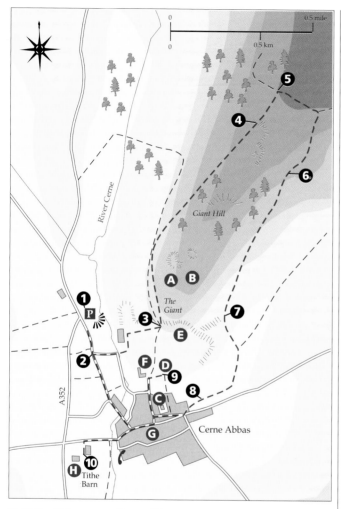

Giant is not officially allowed, but the route of the walk passes under his feet. If you do see anybody venturing closer to the figure known locally as 'His Mightiness', she (for it is more relevant to women) is probably either about to get married or is hoping to become pregnant. The giant is of ancient pagan origin and its survival seems incredible, especially as it had Christian monks living at its feet for centuries. There was an old belief that a living giant who ate human flesh and terrorised the neighbourhood was captured and killed here and that the outline of his huge body was carved in the chalk of the hillside where he lay.

Route description

1 Park your car in the 'Giant View' lay-by off the A352 north of Cerne Abbas. This is 8 miles (12.8 km) north of Dorchester. Cerne Abbas is served by bus (no. 216) from Dorchester and Sherborne. Walk with the giant on your left down the lane towards Cerne Abbas.

2 Turn left along a lane towards the picnic area. Ignore a path beside the River Cerne on your right but go across the bridge to a T-junction. Turn left to walk for 50 yards (45 m) then turn right up the hedged path opposite a barn.

3 Ignore a stile on your left but go ahead across a stile and bear left to pass under the feet of the Giant on your right. Continue parallel with the hedge on your left. Veer right uphill when you reach a path of woodland and a cattle trough on your left.

Until the 19th century Cerne Abbas was a centre for the leather and brewing industries. Nowadays, it is an appealing village with fine buildings, including some timber-fronted cottages and a 15th-century church. It is certainly most famous for its male nude giant carved into the chalk of the nearby hillside.

This walks takes you from Cerne Abbas up on to the downs and past the prehistoric figure of the Cerne Giant on Giant Hill. There is an excellent viewpoint of the Giant at the start of the walk. Access to the

4 Cross the stile in the fence ahead. Keep straight on towards the barn just to the right of the trees on the horizon.

5 Turn right just before the barn to walk with the hedge on your left. Go ahead through a gate in the corner of the field and turn right immediately to go through a gate and walk with the hedge on your right.

6 Veer left when the fence bears right. Follow the clear track downhill.

7 Cross a stile on your right and bear slightly left across the field to a stile near the sports field. Cross it and turn towards the hedge at the bottom, then turn right to walk with the hedge on your left to reach a gate on your left.

8 Go through the gate and turn right along the road (Alton Lane). This leads to Long Street, Cerne Abbas. Ignore Abbey Court on your right but fork right to the parish church of St Mary. Turn right up Abbey Street. Pass the town pond on your right and go on to a gate on your right which leads to the cemetery. Follow the wall on your right and go down to the holy well.

Points of interest

A The Cerne Giant is 180 feet (55 m) high and brandishes a 120 feet (36 m) club. It has survived the centuries by being regularly scoured and tended by the locals, who regard it as safeguarding the fertility of their land. The Giant is now in the care of the National Trust.

It survived the Victorian period intact under the protection of the pioneering archaeologist, General Pitt-Rivers. It is obviously connected with fertility. Making love on the grass of the giant's phallus is a traditional cure for barrenness. Barren women come to just sit on the tip of the phallus, while women about to get married come to walk around the whole figure to ensure a happy marriage. The Giant's association with fertility is strengthened by its link with Beltane, May Day. The eve of Beltane was the time for many to lose their virginity in the woods. A sightline taken vertically up the middle of the phallus on May Day would point directly at the rising sun as it came over the down.

The name Cerne may refer to Cernunnos, the Celtic lord of the wild beasts and a giant who wielded a club. The Giant was most probably adopted by the Romans when Commodus was emperor (180-93 BC). Commodus claimed to be the incarnation of Hercules and assumed the title of Hercules Romanus. Evidence of a lion's skin draped over the Giant's left arm (now overgrown) supports this theory.

B The ancient earthwork above the Giant's outstretched arm is the Trendle or Frying Pan. A flat platform may have had a ceremonial purpose. The Cerne Abbas village May Pole might have stood here. Prisoners may have been kept in the Trendle to await sacrifice in the Beltane fire, perhaps in a wickerwork giant (called a 'kolosson' by the Romans).

C The parish church of St Mary has an imposing 15th-century buttressed tower, a late Norman chancel, heraldic glass and remarkable 14th-century wall paintings. Also splendid gargoyles. Around the church there are ruins of the Abbey of Cerne.

D St Augustine's Well: St Augustine is said to have put his staff into the ground and out flowed water. He named the place Cernel from the Latin 'Cerno' (I see) and Hel (the giant?). Women drink here in the hope of becoming pregnant while a wishing stone has a St Catherine's Wheel carved on it for women to pray for a husband. A ley line passes through this stone and up to the Trendle.

E The old abbey church stood here. A 9th-century monastery was refounded on Benedictine lines in 987 and dissolved by Henry VIII in 1539.

F The sumptuous porch to the now vanished Abbot's Lodging stands in the grounds of Abbey Farm, an impressive gabled Tudor building in flint and stone.

G The abbey's 14th-century Tithe Barn was the prototype of the great barn in which Sergeant Troy led the alcoholic revels in *Far from the Madding Crowd*.

Walk 37
DOGBURY HILL

5.5 miles (8.8 km)   Moderate

This is a splendid route for views, with the path reaching a height of 870 feet (265 m). Good, clear tracks are followed, making this a walk suitable for all (although there may be large puddles after wet weather).
Hardy moved the location of *The Woodlanders* here after its first edition and enough belts of woodland have survived to make this setting authentic.

Route description
1 Park at a lay-by on the A352 road north of Minterne Magna. As you come from Dorchester, which is 10 miles (16 km) to the south, the lay-by is on your right just after a converted schoolhouse. Go through the gate between the schoolhouse and the lay-by and walk ahead to a

66

second gate which is waymarked. Bear slightly left across the field to a stile in the top fence. Cross a narrow field to a gate ahead.

2 Turn right, along the fenced track that is an old ridgeway. After passing through woodland on Dogbury Hill, the path affords splendid views both to the left (over north Dorset and Somerset) and to the right (overlooking Minterne House and the Upper Cerne Valley). Pass a plantation of trees on your right.

3 Just after the end of the fencing on your right and just before the ridgeway bends left, turn right through a gate to follow a grassy track which soon bears left downhill. Emerge from the woodland along a sunken green track which descends to continue along a hedged track which gradually bears right.

4 Go ahead at the cross-tracks, pass a farmyard on your right and a dovecote and the stump of Minterne Parva's old medieval cross on your left. Walk down the lane to the A352.

5 Turn left along the A352 for 200 yards (180 m) then turn right up the lane to Up Cerne.

6 Turn right at the bus shelter to walk with a stream on your right. Continue past the Great Pond which can be glimpsed through the trees on your left. This lane deteriorates to a rough track as it climbs. Ignore a track on your left and go ahead to a metal barn.

7 Go to the right of the barn and walk with the hedge on your right. When this track turns left, go straight ahead across a field towards woodland.

8 Follow the distinct path through the wood and continue across a narrow field to a roadside waymark post.

9 Turn right along this minor road until you reach a corner where the road bends sharply right.

10 Turn left off the road at this corner to follow a hedged, grassy track. Bear right with this track down through woodland. Across the hedge on your left you can catch a glimpse of Somerset.

11 Turn right when you reach another minor road. Follow it until its junction with the A352 at Dogbury Gate, where you turn right to walk very carefully back to your car at the lay-by on your left.

Points of interest

A Minterne Magna replaced Melbury Osmond as Hardy's 'Great Hintock'. The gardens of Minterne House have acres of shrubs and rare trees. In eary summer the gardens are ablaze with rhododendrons and azaleas. The house is not open to the public.

B Minterne Parva is a tiny hamlet with an old dovecote.

C Up Cerne is an attractive hamlet with an excellent manor house and tiny church dating from the 16th century.

D High Stoy is a splendid viewpoint and was one of Hardy's favourite spots. This was the country of *The Woodlanders*. It was also climbed by the four friends in the poem, *Under High Stoy Hill*.

E Dogbury Gate's name refers to the old turnpike gate that used to stand here. Hardy's poem *Life and Death at Sunrise* is set here. From Dogbury Gate the road westwards to Evershot (Walk 38) climbs over Gore Hill, with views down to the prehistoric Cross and Hand, an unusual monolith in an isolated setting. In *Tess of the D'Urbervilles*, Tess is made to swear an oath of fidelity on the stone.

Walk 38
EVERSHOT

5 miles (8 km)   Easy, but sometimes muddy

This is a varied walk starting at Evershot which, at an altitude of 700 feet (180 m), is the second highest village in Dorset. It descends to follow muddy lanes to Melbury Osmond, the home of Hardy's mother. The walk then follows well-surfaced estate driveways past Melbury House and through its deer park. One stretch of the walk is extremely muddy so it is advisable to wear boots.

The scenery on this route is described by Hardy in *The Woodlanders*. It is also the setting for several scenes in *Tess of the D'Urbervilles*.

Route description
1 Start from the grassy triangle at the bottom of the hill in the east end of Evershot. This is both the bus stop (Comfy Lux nos. 211 and 212 between Dorchester, Sherborne and Yeovil) and roadside parking (but keep the driveway to Melbury House clear). Evershot is at a junction of minor roads 1.5 miles (2.4 km) west of the A37 where it crosses the Bristol to Weymouth railway line at Holywell. Walk away from the driveway to Melbury House, passing Back Lane on your right and following the main road as it bends right into Fore Street, passing Summer Lane on your left.

2 Turn right along Back Lane between Tess' Cottage and St Osmond's Church. Follow Back Lane as it bends right to meet the road near your start.

3 Turn left along the road and fork left towards Melbury House.

4 Fork right along an uphill track. Continue through trees and past a water tower on your left at the top of the hill. Walk down to the bottom of the hill, passing conifer trees on your left and a conifer plantation between two fields on your right.

5 Bear left, passing deciduous woodland on your right. When you have a fenced field on your left, look for glimpses of Lucerne Lake through the trees on your right.

6 Just after passing a thatched boathouse on your right, go ahead through a gate and turn right, off the main tracks. Bear left through a gate, cross a stream and bear left through a gate after it.

7 Walk with the fence on your right past a waymark post. At the end of the field, turn right through a small gate and turn left immediately along a track. Continue through a gate to meet a road as it bends towards a house on your left. Go straight across this road to the muddy track opposite. Continue through a gate at the end of this hedged track and cross a corner of a field to a small gate ahead.

8 Continue along the hedged track, which soon bears left to cross a stream and then bear right. Go under an archway where the path is very muddy, before bearing left to emerge between two thatched cottages at the side of a road.

9 Turn right along this road to reach Melbury Osmond and its church. Retrace your steps and continue to enter the parkland of Melbury House. Go ahead along the driveway that is also the public path. Keep straight on towards Melbury House.

10 Just before Melbury House, turn right with the driveway. Follow it as it bends left and uphill through a deer park. Eventually the drive descends to the road at the grassy triangle where you started.

Points of interest

A   The Acorn Inn was renamed the 'Sow and Acorn' in *Tess of the D'Urbervilles*. Tess avoided it, but Tupcombe, Squire Dornell's man, sat in its inglenook in the hope of hearing news of Betty.

B   'Tess' Cottage' is across Back Lane from the church. This is where Tess had breakfast on her way to 'Emminster' (Beaminster) to see Angel's parents. Evershot was renamed 'Evershead' by Hardy. Its real name is derived from the Anglo-Saxon for 'wild boar thicket'. St Osmond's Church was rebuilt in the 19th century but has a Norman font. The poet George Crabbe was rector here from 1783 to 1787.

C   St John's Well is on your right about 200 yards (180 m) from the church down Back Lane. This is the source of the River Frome, which flows through Dorset to reach the sea at Poole Harbour. It was near here that Tess discovered Alec d'Urberville ranting in a barn (now demolished).

D   The mixed deciduous woodland is like that in which Giles Winterborne made his home in a 'one-chimney hut' that so contrasted with nearby Melbury House. Giles had resorted to a deserted charcoal burner's cottage after being evicted from his home. He was unable to renew his lease when it reverted to the landowner after the expiration of a given number of generations. This gloomy image of blighted crops and stunted growth pervades *The Woodlanders*. Such is the natural world, but Hardy also extols nature, with evocative forest scenes. It is to here that Grace Melbury comes, escaping from her faithless husband and seeking Giles' help. She finds 'a square cot of one storey only, sloping up on all sides

to a chimney in the midst . . . the room within was kitchen, parlour and bedchamber all in one; the natural sandstone floor was worn into hills and dales by long treading, so that none of the furniture stood level, and the table slanted like a desk'.

E   Hardy's parents' families had once owned land around Melbury Osmond so it is natural to locate *The Woodlanders*, with its theme of lost status due to loss of property, here. Melbury Osmond was, indeed, the original for Hardy's 'Great Hintock'. Not wishing to offend the Earl of Ilchester, who lived in Melbury House, Hardy tried to move the location further east in the novel's second edition. Melbury Osmond now became 'King's Hintock'. The last scene of *The Woodlanders* is still definitely set in Melbury Osmond, however, with Marty in the moonlight beside Giles' grave in 'Great Hintock' churchyard. This church was where Hardy's parents, Thomas Hardy (senior) and Jemima Hand, were married on 22nd December 1839. Hardy's mother used to live in the thatched cottage on the north side of the church.

F   Melbury House was originally Hardy's 'Hintock House' but it became 'King's Hintock Court' in the second edition of *The Woodlanders*. In reality it is a manor house built by Sir Giles Strangways shortly before 1540. It is now a stud farm for racehorses.

G   Melbury Park was Hardy's 'King's Hintock Park', and your route is along the tree-lined driveway that the enigmatic stranger used in *The Duke's Reappearance*. Look out for three types of deer here – red, fallow and Japanese sika. The private drive is a public path.

Walk 39
EGGARDON HILL & POWERSTOCK COMMON 7 miles (11.8 km) Easy

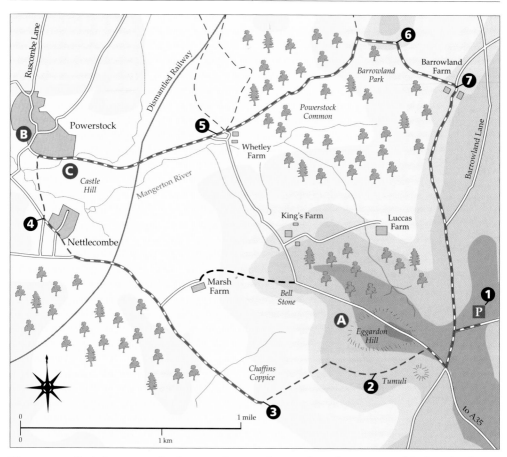

There are excellent views across the downs and over to the coast from the ramparts of the Iron Age fort on Eggardon Hill. The walk descends below the earthworks of the fort into a valley and crosses fields, tracks and lanes before reaching the picturesque village of Powerstock. You then pass through the woodlands of Powerstock Common to return to Eggardon Hill.

Route description

1 Start from the car park just off the lane that runs past Eggardon Hill. Follow the lane turning left at the T-junction and right at the next junction signposted to Powerstock and West Milton. Go through the waymarked gate on the left and follow the direction of the blue arrow towards the fort. Go through a metal gate and follow the track for a few yards.

2 Bear left in front of another metal gate. Ahead are two stiles: climb the right-hand one to explore the fort; to continue the walk, climb the left-hand stile and follow the grassy track downhill, keeping the wire fence to your left and the earthworks of the fort to your right. Turn sharp left and go through a metal gate taking the path downhill between the hedges. Pass through a gate into an open field, keeping a hedge on your right. Go through another gate and then turn right in front of farm buildings on to a rough track.

3 Follow this track for about 1 mile (1.5 km). The track becomes a tarmac lane passing under a disused railway bridge. A few yards ahead, turn right through a gate, then turn left over a stile and walk diagonally across a field towards a gate in the far corner. Pass through this gate and climb the stone stile leading on to a lane. Turn right into Nettlecombe.

4 Bear left at the first junction and right at the next junction, passing through a gate at the public footpath sign to Powerstock. Ahead is a lovely view of the village. Keep to the wire fence on the right-hand side of the field. Where the fence bears right, continue straight on, descending steeply into a valley. Go through a gate, cross a footbridge over a stream, and bear slightly right across a meadow to go through another gate. Cross another bridge and follow the path uphill to the lane, keeping a wall on your left and a hedge on your right. Follow the lane for about 1 mile (1.5 km). Where the path bears to the right by the bridleway sign to Stones Common, go straight on towards the gate.

5 Go through the gate and pass in front of a farmhouse. Go through a metal gate and walk straight ahead. Go through another gate to enter woodland and follow a path through a conifer plantation. Bear right uphill through broad-leaved woodland. At the top of the wood bear right along a track to emerge into an area of open grassland and bracken on the right-hand edge of the trees.

6 A few yards to the right, go through a blue-waymarked gate and walk in a straight line across the field ahead. On the far side turn right by a wire fence and head towards a metal gate in the bottom corner. Pass through the gate and continue uphill along a track to Barrowland Farm, here going through two metal gates in quick succession.

7 Turn right along a track, keeping the farmhouse on your right. At the end of the farm buildings continue straight ahead, passing through a metal gate and heading diagonally uphill across a field to go through a gate in the top right-hand corner. Bear right along the right-hand edge of a field, by a wire fence and above a steep wooded bank on the right. Where the field edge curves to the right, continue in the same direction across the field, making for a metal gate about half-way along its far edge (crops may force you to keep to the fence instead). Go through the gate, turn left and go through another gate leading onto the lane. Turn right and after half a mile (0.75 km) turn left at the first junction to return to the car park.

Points of interest

A   Eggardon Hill is over 800 feet (240 m) high. The fort is one of the most impressive of all the Iron Age forts in Dorset. It has three banks with intermediate ditches and additional defences at the east and north-west entrances. The visible hollows in the internal area are grain storage pits. There are also two Bronze Age round barrows within the defences.

B   Powerstock is one of the most picturesque villages in the county with its winding lanes full of stone and thatched cottages. In 1968 the BBC made a documentary about Powerstock as it was decided that it was the village least changed by the 20th century. Powerstock's Church of St Mary was mostly rebuilt in 1859, but still retains an ornamented Norman chancel arch from the original 12th-century structure. The 15th-century south doorway is flanked by carved figures in canopied niches. The church school, just down the road, was built in 1848 from bits of a demolished medieval chapel. Its doorway is 12th century.

C   You can still see the turf-covered motte and bailey of the Norman castle that once stood here.

D   This is a remnant of medieval Powerstock Forest, which was made into a royal forest by King John and is now a Dorset Naturalists' Trust Reserve.

Walk 40
GOLDEN CAP

3 miles (4.8 km)   Strenuous

This is a walk over the highest cliff on the south coast. The scenery is dramatic and the views are extensive, from Chesil Beach and the Isle of Portland in the east, to Lyme Regis and Devon in the west.

Route description

1 Start from the car park (charge) near the beach of Seatown. This is at the end of Sea Hill Lane, which runs south from the A35 opposite the church in Chideock. This is on the Southern National's 31 & X31 bus routes between Weymouth and Taunton. As you face the sea, turn right to keep it on your left. Follow the signposted Dorset Coast Path, which climbs away from the beach towards Golden Cap.

2 Walk with the fence on your right, then follow the well-trodden path through scrubland. Cross a bar stile and bear left along the signposted Coast Path across an open field to a signpost beside a bench. Continue to reach a signposted stile in the fence on your left. Cross it to follow the path to the summit of Golden Cap.

3 Follow the path from the Ordnance Survey triangulation pillar to the memorial stone to Lord Antrim. Continue downhill to a signpost, where you bear right downhill to a ruined church (St Gabriel's).

4 Retrace your steps and fork left steeply uphill to follow the signposted bridleway. Keep the hedge on your left until you go through a gate and walk right around the edge of this field to a gate in its far top corner. Follow the signposted bridleway to Langdon Hill and Seatown.

5 Go ahead through a gate and bear right along the edge of the wood on Langdon Hill. Turn right over a stile at a sign marked 'footpath' to follow the path to Seatown, which follows a fence on your left to rejoin the Coast Path at a signpost. Turn left through the scrubland.

6 Bear left near the end of this scrubland to a waymarked gate. (If you prefer, follow the coastal path back to the car park.) Follow the yellow arrow to a hedged path ahead. Cross a footbridge to bear right across a field to a waymarked bar stile. Walk down a narrow path to a stile which gives access to Sea Hill Lane. Turn right to reach the car park.

Points of interest

A Seatown is situated in a gap in the cliffs overlooking a shingle beach. It has an 18th-century inn.

B At 618 feet (188 m), Golden Cap is the highest cliff along the south coast. It is named after its flat summit of golden sandstone. The National Trust has achieved the conservation of 6 miles (9.6 km) of rugged cliffs in its Golden Cap Estate. Lord Antrim, the chairman of the National Trust from 1966 until his death in 1977, is remembered with a memorial at the summit.

C The ruined church at Stanton St Gabriel testifies to the former existence of a thriving community here. There were 23 families living in cottages around the village green in 1650, but the population gradually shifted to nearby Morcombelake. Finally, in 1824, the road was re-routed through Morcombelake.